Some comments from our readers...

"I have to praise you and your company on the fine products you turn out. I have twelve of the *Teach Yourself VISUALLY* and *Simplified* books in my house. They were instrumental in helping me pass a difficult computer course. Thank you for creating books that are easy to follow."

—*Gordon Justin (Brielle, NJ)*

"I commend your efforts and your success. I teach in an outreach program for the Dr. Eugene Clark Library in Lockhart, TX. Your *Teach Yourself VISUALLY* books are incredible and I use them in my computer classes. All my students love them!"

—*Michele Schalin (Lockhart, TX)*

"Thank you so much for helping people like me learn about computers. The Maran family is just what the doctor ordered. Thank you, thank you, thank you."

—*Carol Moten (New Kensington, PA)*

"I would like to take this time to compliment maranGraphics on creating such great books. Thank you for making it clear. Keep up the good work."

—*Kirk Santoro (Burbank, CA)*

"I write to extend my thanks and appreciation for your books. They are clear, easy to follow, and straight to the point. Keep up the good work!

—*Seward Kollie (Dakar, Senegal)*

"What fantastic teaching books you have produced! Congratulations to you and your staff. You deserve the Nobel prize in Education in the Software category. Thanks for helping me to understand computers."

—*Bruno Tonon (Melbourne, Australia)*

"Over time, I have bought a number of your 'Read Less – Learn More' books. For me, they are THE way to learn anything easily."

—*José A. Mazón (Cuba, NY)*

"I was introduced to maranGraphics about four years ago and YOU ARE THE GREATEST THING THAT EVER HAPPENED TO INTRODUCTORY COMPUTER BOOKS!"

—*Glenn Nettleton (Huntsville, AL)*

"Compliments To The Chef!! Your books are extraordinary! Or, simply put, Extra-Ordinary, meaning way above the rest! THANK YOU THANK YOU THANK YOU! for creating these.

—*Christine J. Manfrin (Castle Rock, CO)*

"I'm a grandma who was pushed by an 11-year-old grandson to join the myself hopelessl until I discovere expert by any mear along than I would you!"

—*Carol Louthain (Logansport, IN)*

"Thank you, thank you, thank you....for making it so easy for me to break into this high-tech world. I now own four of your books. I recommend them to anyone who is a beginner like myself. Now....if you could just do one for programming VCRs, it would make my day!"

—*Gay O'Donnell (Calgary, Alberta, Canada)*

"You're marvelous! I am greatly in your debt."

—*Patrick Baird (Lacey, WA)*

maranGraphics is a family-run business located near Toronto, Canada.

At **maranGraphics**, we believe in producing great computer books — one book at a time.

maranGraphics has been producing high-technology products for over 25 years, which enables us to offer the computer book community a unique communication process.

Our computer books use an integrated communication process, which is very different from the approach used in other computer books. Each spread is, in essence, a flow chart — the text and screen shots are totally incorporated into the layout of the spread.

Introductory text and helpful tips complete the learning experience.

maranGraphics' approach encourages the left and right sides of the brain to work together — resulting in faster orientation and greater memory retention.

Above all, we are very proud of the handcrafted nature of our books. Our carefully-chosen writers are experts in their fields, and spend countless hours researching and organizing the content for each topic. Our artists rebuild every screen shot to provide the best clarity possible, making our

screen shots the most precise and easiest to read in the industry. We strive for perfection, and believe that the time spent handcrafting each element results in the best computer books money can buy.

Thank you for purchasing this book. We hope you enjoy it!

Sincerely,

Robert Maran
President
maranGraphics
Rob@maran.com
www.maran.com
www.hungryminds.com/visual

CREDITS

Acquisitions, Editorial, and Media Development

Project Editor
Timothy J. Borek

Acquisitions Editor
Jen Dorsey

Product Development Supervisor
Lindsay Sandman

Copy Editor
Jill Mazurczyk

Technical Editor
Dennis R. Short

Editorial Manager
Rev Mengle

Editorial Assistant
Amanda Foxworth

Production

Book Design
maranGraphics®

Production Coordinator
Maridee Ennis

Layout and Graphics
Melanie DesJardins, LeAndra Johnson,
Kristin McMullan, Barry Offringa, Betty Schulte

Screen Artists
Mark Harris, Jill A. Proll

Illustrators
Ronda David-Burroughs, David Gregory,
Sean Johannesen, Russ Marini, Steven Schaerer

Proofreaders
Joanne Keaton

Quality Control
John Bitter, Carl Pierce, Linda Quigley,
Dwight Ramsey, Marianne Santy

Indexer
Richard Shrout

Special Help
Judy Maran

ACKNOWLEDGMENTS

General and Administrative

Hungry Minds Technology Publishing Group: Richard Swadley, Vice President & Executive Group Publisher;
Bob Ipsen, Vice President & Executive Publisher; Joe Wikert, Vice President & Publisher; Barry Pruett,
Vice President & Publisher; Mary Bednarek, Editorial Director; Andy Cummings, Editorial Director

Hungry Minds Production for Branded Press: Debbie Stailey, Production Director

ABOUT THE AUTHOR

Sherry Willard Kinkoph has written more than 40 books covering a variety of computer topics ranging from hardware to software, from Microsoft Office programs to the Internet. Her recent titles include *Teach Yourself VISUALLY Flash 5, Master VISUALLY Dreamweaver 4 and Flash 5, and Master VISUALLY FrontPage 2002*. Sherry's never-ending quest is to help users of all levels master the ever-changing computer technologies. No matter how many times software manufacturers and hardware conglomerates throw out a new version or upgrade, Sherry vows to be there to make sense of it all and help computer users get the most out of their machines.

AUTHOR'S ACKNOWLEDGMENTS

Special thanks go out to acquisitions editor Jennifer Dorsey, for handing me such a fun book to tackle; to project editor Tim Borek, for shepherding the book from start to finish, never missing a beat; to copy editor Jill Mazurczyk, for ensuring that all the i's were dotted and t's were crossed; to technical editor Dennis Short, for checking everything over for accuracy and offering his skilled observations; and finally, to the production team at Hungry Minds for their efforts in creating such a visual masterpiece.

To my husband, Greg, for his ongoing support and
enthusiasm for all things computer related.

TABLE OF CONTENTS

Chapter 1

GETTING TO KNOW PREMIERE

Chapter 2

STARTING A PREMIERE PROJECT

Frame Rate: 30fpm
QuickTime editing mode
Frame Size: 320x240

Chapter 3

CAPTURING VIDEO

Chapter 4

IMPORTING PRODUCTION ELEMENTS

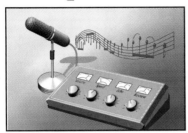

Chapter 5

WORKING WITH CLIPS

Chapter 6

WORKING WITH THE TIMELINE

TABLE OF CONTENTS

Chapter 7

EDITING IN THE MONITOR WINDOW

Chapter 8

EDITING CLIPS IN THE TIMELINE

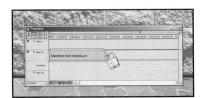

Chapter 9 FINE-TUNING A PROGRAM

Chapter 10 EDITING AUDIO

TABLE OF CONTENTS

Chapter 11

CREATING TRANSITION EFFECTS

Chapter 12

CREATING TEXT AND GRAPHIC EFFECTS

Chapter 13

CREATING VIDEO EFFECTS

Chapter 14

SUPERIMPOSING CLIPS

Chapter 15

CREATING MOTION EFFECTS

Chapter 16

OUTPUTTING DIGITAL VIDEO

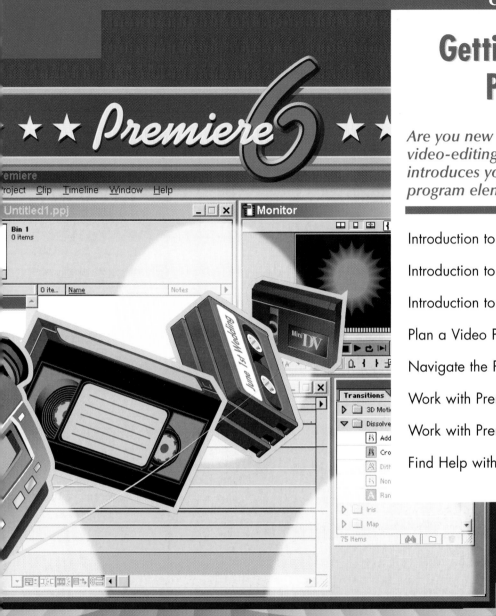

CHAPTER 1

Getting to Know Premiere

Are you new to Premiere and digital video-editing techniques? This chapter introduces you to key concepts and program elements for getting started.

INTRODUCTION TO PREMIERE

You can use Adobe Premiere to edit digital video on your computer. Whether you are using a Mac or a PC, Premiere can help you create dynamic movies and presentations that can be output to other sources, such as videotape or the Web.

What Can I Do with Premiere?

Premiere is a *nonlinear* editing program, which means that you can assemble a video project much like you assemble documents using other types of editing software. You can use Premiere to assemble and edit moving images.

Gather Production Elements

You can import production elements, called *clips*, from other sources, such as video or audio files, and assemble them into a video project in Premiere. You can also capture digital video footage using a camcorder and bring the images into Premiere. See Chapters 3 and 4 to learn more.

Arrange the Clips

Digital editing involves arranging the clips into an actual video that you can output to another source. With Premiere, you can control where a clip starts and stops, rearrange its place on the program timeline, and preview the results to see how the project is progressing. See Chapters 5 through 9 to learn how to work with and edit clips.

Logical order — audio & titles last

Add Video Effects

You can add *transition* effects, such as dissolves and wipes, to move from one scene to another. Premiere offers 75 customizable transition effects for you to apply. You can also create transparency effects that enable you to superimpose one clip over another. See Chapters 11 and 14 to learn more about transitions and superimposing.

Add Titles and Graphics

You can create titles with Premiere's titling feature. You can also add graphics from other programs or draw simple graphic objects and text objects using the Premiere drawing tools. Premiere also provides tools for creating motion effects to make graphics or text move around the video's frames. See Chapter 12 to learn how to add titles and graphics.

Mix Audio

You can record audio from a microphone to use in your video, or you can import audio files from other sources. You can then edit the audio using Premiere's audio mixer. You can create audio effects such as cross-fades and pans. See Chapter 10 to learn more about using audio in Premiere.

Export Your Project

You can export the finished video to a variety of formats, such as Web file formats, files that can be viewed by other programs, and videotape. You can even export your project to an Edit Decision List to send off to a professional production house. See Chapter 16 to learn how to export your projects.

INTRODUCTION TO DIGITAL VIDEO

Digital video format is a high-quality imaging format. The term itself describes video signals stored in a digital form. If you are new to digital video, take a moment to familiarize yourself the fundamentals of this format and the hardware used to create and edit digital media.

Analog versus Digital

Prior to digital media equipment, video content was analog in format. Motion picture film and audio cassette tape are two examples. Today's digital video format, called DV for short, offers higher-quality imaging. You cannot use analog media in Premiere without first digitizing it.

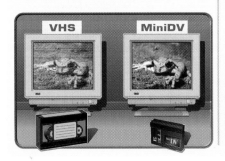

Recording Digital Media

One way to digitize media is to shoot it yourself using a digital camcorder. MiniDV camcorders record the highest quality digital images, followed by Digital 8 (D8) camcorders. If your camcorder has i.Link or FireWire output and your computer has an IEEE 1394 port, you can transfer the video directly into Premiere.

What Is IEEE 1394?

IEEE 1394 is a standard for transferring digital information between peripheral devices, such as a DV camcorder, and your computer. This standard is also referred to by the trade names *FireWire* (Apple Computer) or *i.Link* (Sony Corp.). With an IEEE 1394 cable and port, you can also use Premiere's device control feature to control your camcorder from within Premiere.

Digitizing Analog Media

You can also use analog camcorders, such as 8mm or Hi8, if you have the necessary computer hardware, such as a capture card or capture board, for converting the analog signals to digital. Many types of analog capture cards can help you convert analog video from various sources, including VHS tapes.

Enhanced Editing Setups

For more advanced editing setups, you may include a DV deck for dedicated playback and recording, a professional-quality NTSC monitor, and a high-quality speaker system.

Requirements for DV

To make the most of Premiere 6 and digital video, your computer system needs to meet some minimum requirements, such as processor power and a FireWire or IEEE 1394 interface. For more information, see the listed system requirements at www.adobe.com/products/premiere/systemreqs.html.

Editing Requirements

Digital video consumes a great deal of space. To store one hour of digital video on your computer's hard drive, you need 12.9 gigabytes (GB) of free space. Keep this in mind when storing video clips on your hard drive. The more clips you add, the more space they take up. Large-capacity hard drives work best for digital video editing.

INTRODUCTION TO VIDEO EDITING

Editing video is like putting together pieces of a puzzle. As the editor, you decide where each clip goes and how long it plays. If you are new to the world of video editing, take a few moments to acquaint yourself with how editing is handled in Premiere.

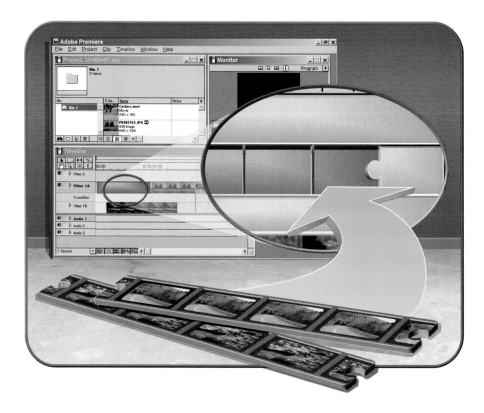

Traditional Video Editing

Traditional video editing requires expensive editing equipment and a production facility. Editors cue videotapes to edit points, copy scenes from various tapes to a master tape, and assemble a project sequentially. The process is time-consuming and tedious. If the editor decides they need to add a new clip in the middle of the program, the entire video must be remastered.

Digital Editing with Premiere

Premiere combines features commonly found in a roomful of video-editing equipment into one program you can use on your computer or laptop. Rather than deal with videotapes, you can create a project by importing or capturing clips and then assembling them in an order that best suits your project. If you need to add a clip later, you can easily insert it where it is needed.

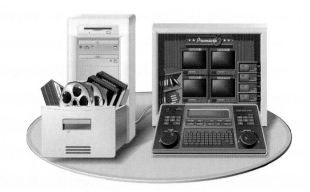

Editing Methods

Premiere provides two main ways to edit a video. You can use the Timeline window or the Monitor window. Use the Timeline window to arrange the clips you want to appear in the video by tracks, and use the Monitor window to fine-tune the video. To learn more about editing with the Timeline and Monitor windows, see Chapters 6 through 9.

Editing Workspace

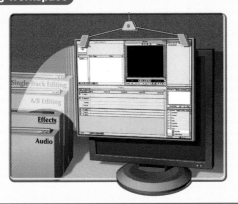

Premiere offers four workspace scenarios for you to create and edit your project: Single-Track Editing, A/B Editing, Effects, and Audio. The workspace you choose depends on what types of edits you are performing. For example, you may choose A/B Editing if you want to drag clips onto the Timeline. You can learn more about workspace in Chapter 2.

Plan Ahead with a Storyboard

Premiere also offers a storyboarding feature to help you plan out your project and the edits you want to make. With the Storyboard feature, you can visualize how your project scenes appear. When you finalize your project, you can then place the clips in the timeline. Learn how to create a storyboard in Chapter 2.

PLAN A VIDEO PROJECT

To make the best use of your time and effort spent editing a video project with Premiere, start by defining the process you want to use to achieve your goals. Use the tips in this task to help plan out pre-production steps and choose an editing strategy.

Pre-production Plan
"CPR for Beginners"
- Project outline
- Script development
- Storyboard
- Equipm...

Pre-Production Planning

Most of your project planning occurs in pre-production. Outline, script, or storyboard your video concept. If your video includes a cast of people, plan out roles and costuming. Pre-production planning also includes establishing locations, budgets, sets and props.

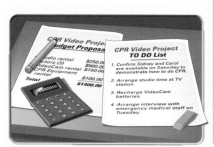

Outline

Always take time to outline your video project in some fashion, even if it is a simple paper outline of scenes, shots, or goals. An outline can help you organize your project as well as identify what items you need to complete the project.

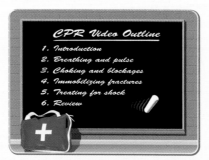

Script

If your video project includes speaking parts or narration, take time to finalize a script before shooting your video and keep the script handy as you edit clips. Formal scripts are another good tool to help you organize your project and materials needed during the shoot.

Storyboard

To really help you visualize your video recordings, sketch out key actions needed for the project. A storyboard looks much like a comic strip, with frames showing changes in action. A storyboard may include notes about sound, camera angles, and direction.

Production

Production refers to the actual shooting of your raw video footage. Things to consider during production are lighting, sound, camera angles, and *blocking* — the movement of people in the scenes.

Choose an Export Format

Decide what format you want to save your project to and make sure all the settings in Premiere comply with the specifications for that format. For example, if you are creating a project that will be broadcast on the Web, determine early on what frame size and rate you will use. Setting up your project correctly for export before you begin can save you numerous problems later.

NAVIGATE THE PROGRAM WINDOW

The Premiere interface is focused on three main areas: the Project window, the Monitor window, and the Timeline window. In addition, palettes are also used to present commands and effects you can apply to your project.

The Premiere window as it looks on a PC.

Project Window

Use this window to manage the contents of your video, including all the clips and titles.

Monitor Window

Use this window to view and edit clips. Depending on the workspace settings you have applied, the Monitor window may show both the Source and Program monitors.

Timeline Window

Use this window to see the tracks – the linear representations of media added to a project – that comprise your video and how they relate to other clips. You can also perform edits in the Timeline window.

Palette Windows

Premiere uses palettes to present additional commands and options you can apply to your project. Premiere provides eight palettes you can view, and some share the same palette window as others.

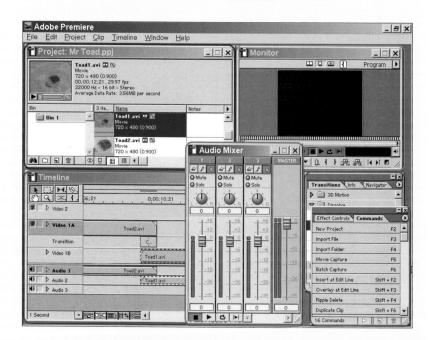

Audio Mixer

Use the Audio Mixer window to edit sounds in your video project.

The Premiere window as it looks on a Mac.

Project Window

Use this window to manage the contents of your video, including all the clips and titles.

Monitor Window

Use this window to view and edit clips. Depending on the workspace settings you have applied, the Monitor window may show both the Source and Program monitors.

Timeline Window

Use this window to see the tracks – the linear representations of media added to a project – that comprise your video and how they relate to other clips. You can also perform edits in the Timeline window.

Palette Windows

Premiere uses palettes to present additional commands and options you can apply to your project. Premiere provides eight palettes you can view, and some share the same palette window as others.

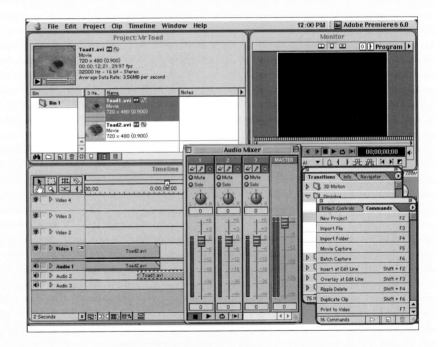

Audio Mixer

Use the Audio Mixer window to edit sounds in your video project.

WORK WITH PREMIERE WINDOWS

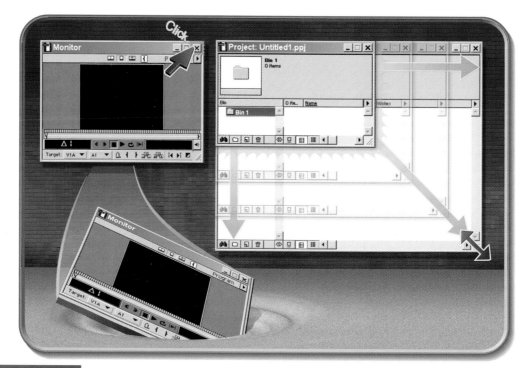

You can open, close, move, and resize the various windows within the Premiere program window. For example, you may want to close the Timeline window to better focus on organizing clips in the Project window, or you may need to resize the Monitor window to better view your video.

WORK WITH PREMIERE WINDOWS

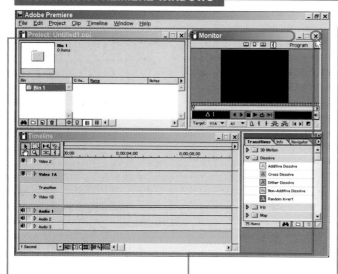

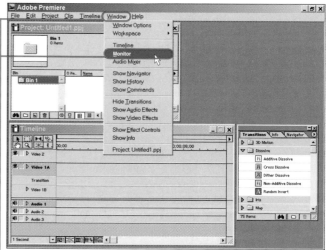

CLOSE A WINDOW

1 Click the title bar of the window you want to close.

2 Click the window's **Close** button (⊠ in Windows and ☐ on a Mac).

■ The window is removed from the screen.

OPEN A WINDOW

1 Click **Window**.

2 Click the name of the window you want to display.

■ Premiere opens the window.

Note: You can have numerous primary and secondary windows open at the same time. Too many open windows, however, crowd the screen.

How do I move the Project window out of the way without closing the entire project file?

You cannot close the Project window without closing the entire video file. To move the Project window out of the way, you can minimize it, making it look like a title bar at the bottom of the program window.

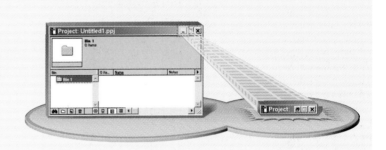

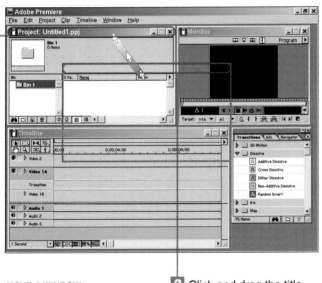

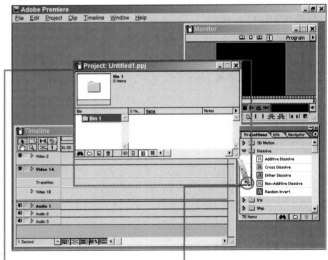

MOVE A WINDOW

1 Click the title bar of the window you want to move.

■ The window appears active.

2 Click and drag the title bar to a new location on the screen.

■ The window is moved.

RESIZE A WINDOW

1 Click the title bar of the window you want to resize.

■ The window appears active.

2 Click and drag the window's corner or border.

■ The window is resized.

You can use the Premiere palettes to access commands and other features to help you edit your video project. To save space, several palettes are grouped into a single window, and you display each palette by clicking the tabs at the top of the palette window.

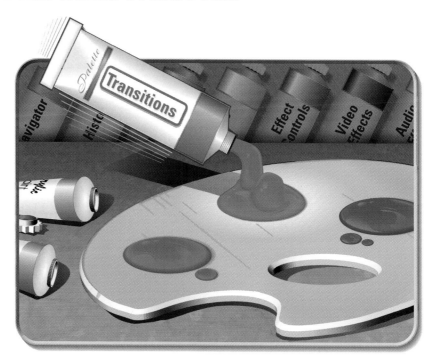

WORK WITH PREMIERE PALETTES

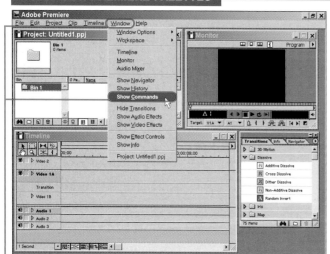

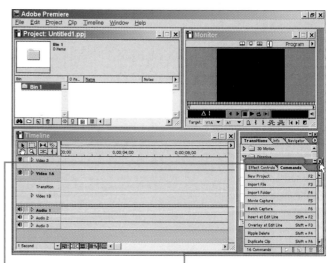

OPEN A PALETTE

◼ Click **Window**.

◼ Click the name of the palette you want to display.

◼ Premiere opens the palette.

Note: If a palette containing the features you want to use is already open, simply click the tab you want to display.

CLOSE A PALETTE

◼ Click the top bar of the palette window you want to close.

◼ Click ☒ (Windows) or ▢ (Mac) to close the palette.

◼ The palette vanishes from the screen.

Can I rearrange the Premiere palettes?

Yes. You can move a palette from one palette window and place it in another, or you can drag a palette out from one palette window into a window of its own. Open both the palette window containing the palette you want to move and the palette window you want to move to, then drag the palette's tab from one window and drop it into the other.

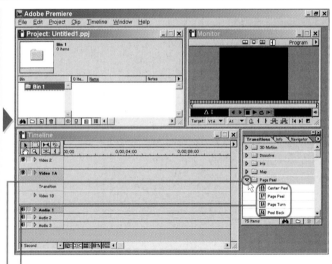

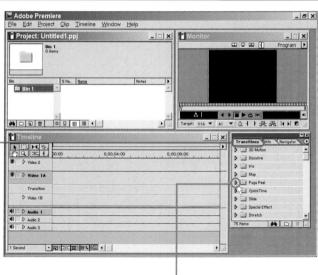

VIEW PALETTE
FOLDER CONTENTS

1 Click the palette tab you want to view.

■ The palette is displayed in front of the other palettes in the group.

2 Click the arrow in front of the folder you want to view.

■ You can also double-click the folder name.

■ The folder's contents appear listed beneath the folder name.

■ To hide the folder contents, click the arrow in front of the folder.

■ You can also double-click the folder name.

FIND HELP WITH PREMIERE

You can use Premiere's Help feature to quickly find assistance with a task or procedure. Premiere comes with offline Web page files listing various Help topics.

You can find sample movie files to study in the Sample Folder within the Premiere 6.0 folder.

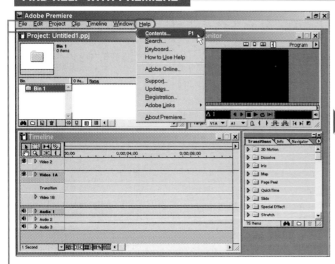

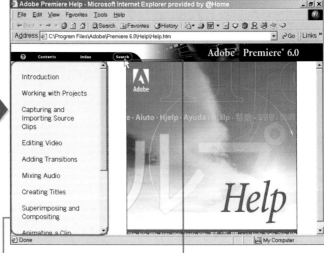

1 Click **Help**.

2 Click **Contents**.

■ Your Web browser immediately launches and displays an offline Web page.

■ You can scroll through the topics and follow links to the information you want.

3 To search for a specific Premiere topic, click the **Search** link.

■ A search page opens.

Where else can I find Premiere help?

The Adobe Web site (www. adobe.com/products/premiere) is a good place to start if you are looking for additional information about the Premiere program. Another way to access the site is to click **Help**, and then **Adobe Online**.

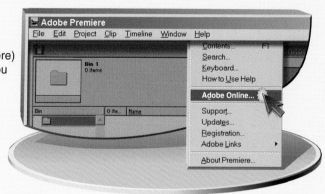

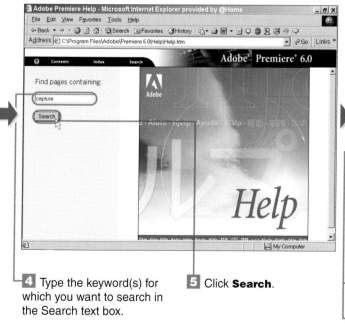

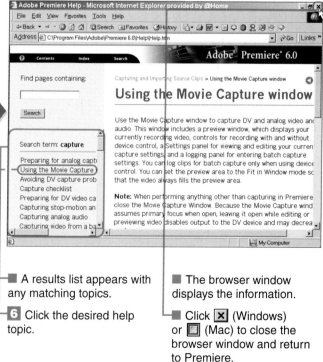

■4 Type the keyword(s) for which you want to search in the Search text box.

■5 Click **Search**.

■ A results list appears with any matching topics.

■6 Click the desired help topic.

■ The browser window displays the information.

■ Click ⊠ (Windows) or ▢ (Mac) to close the browser window and return to Premiere.

Premiere Settings

- Workspace Settings
- Project Settings
- Frame Rate
- Frame Size
- Compression
- Presets

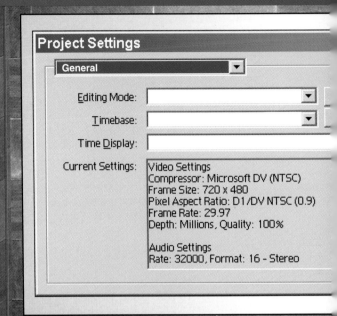

Project Settings

General

Editing Mode:

Timebase:

Time Display:

Current Settings:
```
Video Settings
Compressor: Microsoft DV (NTSC)
Frame Size: 720 x 480
Pixel Aspect Ratio: D1/DV NTSC (0.9)
Frame Rate: 29.97
Depth: Millions, Quality: 100%

Audio Settings
Rate: 32000, Format: 16 - Stereo
```

Frame Rate

CHAPTER 2

Starting a Premiere Project

To begin working on a video project in Premiere, you must take time to establish your project settings. This chapter shows you how to get started.

UNDERSTANDING PREMIERE SETTINGS

You can use the various workspace and project settings in Premiere to tell the program how to handle video and audio as you edit. When determining project settings, consider both your source material and the output of your project.

```
Frame Rate: 30fpm
QuickTime editing mode
Frame Size: 320x240
```

Workspace Settings

Premiere's workspace settings control the screen's editing layout. Use *A/B editing* to view multiple tracks, including transitions. With A/B editing, you can edit video by dragging clips to the Timeline and see additonal tracks for transitions. Use *Single-Track editing* to perform more sophisticated edits using the Source and the Project areas in the Monitor window.

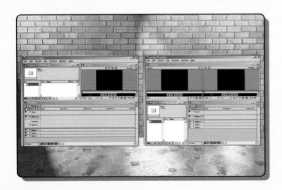

Project Settings

Premiere's project settings fall into five categories: General, Video, Audio, Keyframe and Rendering, and Capture. You can set project settings at the beginning of a project, or you can fine-tune them when you are ready to output the project. Project settings include everything from frame rate and size to audio controls. You can even save a set of project settings as a file you can then load into a new project.

Frame Rate

Frame rate determines the smoothness of motion during video playback. The standard frame rate for film is 24 frames per second, and the standard for video is 30 frames per second. Video with higher frame rates appears more fluid. Slower frame rates, however, download more quickly from the Web. Consider your project's output when determining frame rate.

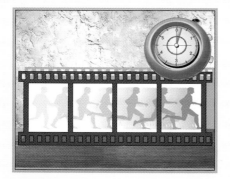

Frame Size

Frame size controls the width and height of your video playback. Frame size is measured in pixels. Several standards, including NTSC (U.S.) and PAL (Europe), exist for videotape output and digital video. If outputting for the Web, keep in mind that the bigger the frame size, the longer it takes to download.

Compression

Video requires large amounts of storage space, but you can reduce the file size by applying a *compression* scheme. You control compression in Premiere by designating a *codec* (short for "*co*mpression" and "*dec*ompression"). The computer and the hardware you use determines what codecs are available. QuickTime and AVI are two popular codecs.

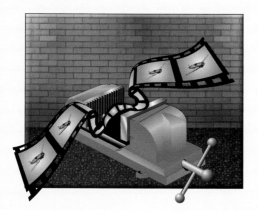

Presets

Premiere includes built-in presets you can use as your project settings. The Presets available cover common types of video source footage, including DV footage for the NTSC (U.S.) standard as well as the PAL (Europe) standard.

SET AN INITIAL WORKSPACE

You can choose a workspace to use when editing in Premiere when you start the program for the very first time. A workspace determines the layout of the editing windows. You can choose between A/B editing or Single-Track editing. The choice you make becomes the default workspace for subsequent launches of the program.

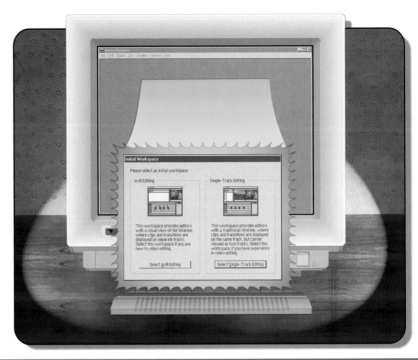

SET AN INITIAL WORKSPACE

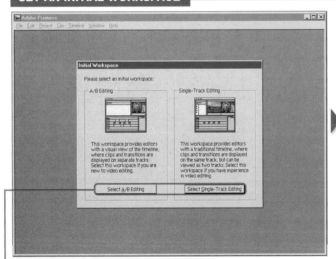

1 Open the Premiere program window.

■ The first time you launch Premiere, the Initial Workspace dialog box appears.

2 Click an editing option.

■ For basic editing, click **Select A/B Editing**.

■ For more complex editing tasks, click **Select Single-Track Editing**.

■ The Load Project Settings dialog box appears.

Note: See the section "Navigate Project Settings" to learn more about the various settings.

3 Click **OK**.

■ Premiere opens the associated editing environment.

Note: The next time you launch the program, Premiere uses the initial editing layout you chose.

CHANGE WORKSPACE SETTINGS

You may want to change workspace settings from one project to the next. Choose A/B editing for basic editing, or Single-Track editing for more complex editing tasks.

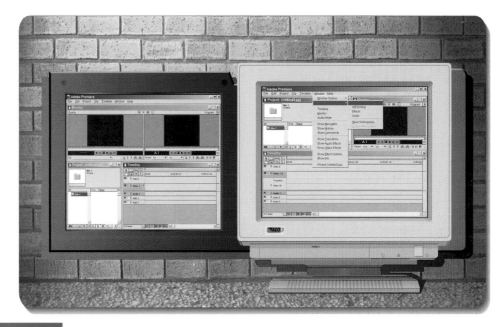

CHANGE WORKSPACE SETTINGS

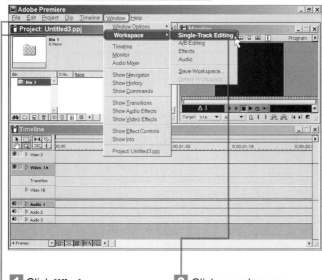

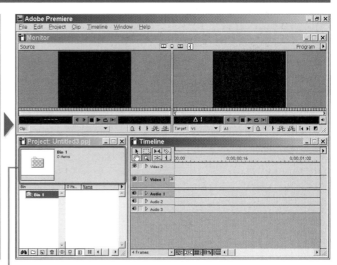

1 Click **Window**.

2 Click **Workspace**.

3 Click a workspace setting.

Note: Single-Track and A/B editing are the main video editing layouts.

■ Premiere displays the workspace setting you specified.

■ This example shows the Single-Track editing workspace.

Note: You can resize the various windows as needed by clicking and dragging the window borders.

SAVE A PROJECT

You can save a project file and assign it a unique name for reusing it later. Premiere saves project files in the PPJ file format. When you save a project, it includes references to source files as well as all of your recent edits. Project files are much smaller in size than source files.

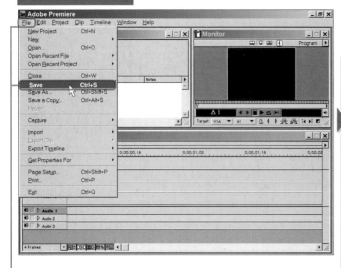

1 Click **File**.

2 Click **Save**.

■ The Save File dialog box appears.

■ To save an existing file under a new filename, click the **Save As** command.

3 Type a name for the file.

■ Click here to locate a different folder or drive in which to save to the file.

4 Click **Save**.

■ Premiere saves the project file.

Note: To save changes to an existing project, click **File**, *then* **Save**.

CLOSE A PROJECT

You can close a project
when you want to start a
new project or when you
want to close the
Premiere program
window. You can have
only one project open at
a time in Premiere.

CLOSE A PROJECT

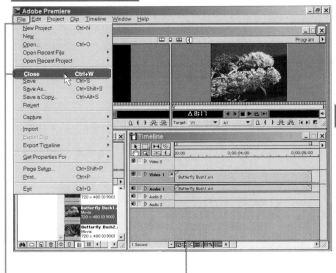

■1 Click **File**.

■2 Click **Close**.

■ You can also click the
Project Window's [X]
(Windows) or [□] (Mac) to
close the project.

■ If you have not saved your
work, Premiere prompts you
to do so. Click **Yes** to save,
No to close without saving,
or **Cancel** to abort the
action.

*Note: To close the program window
entirely, click **File**, then **Exit**.*

START A NEW PROJECT

You can start a new project at any time. By default, Premiere opens a new project using the default presets whenever you launch the program.

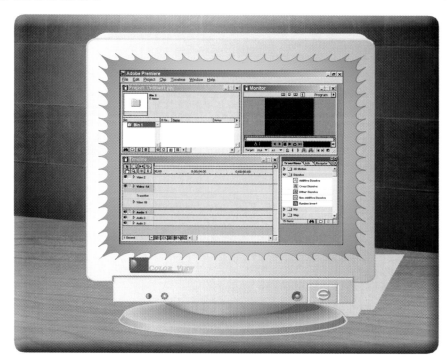

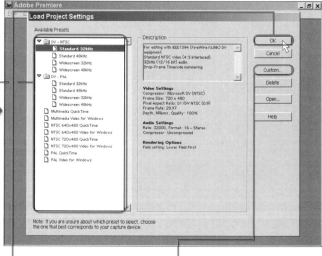

1 Click **File**.

2 Click **New Project**.

■ The Load Project Settings dialog box appears.

3 Click **OK** to use the default settings.

■ To use another preset, click the preset from the list before clicking **OK**.

■ To customize the settings, click here.

■ Premiere opens a new project file onscreen.

OPEN AN EXISTING PROJECT

You can open an existing
project at any time. Only
one project is allowed to
be open at a time in
Premiere. Be sure to
save your current project
before opening another
project file.

OPEN AN EXISTING PROJECT

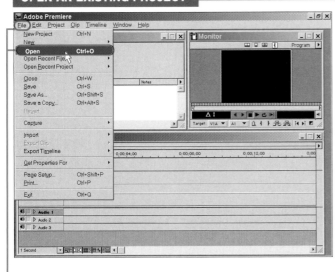

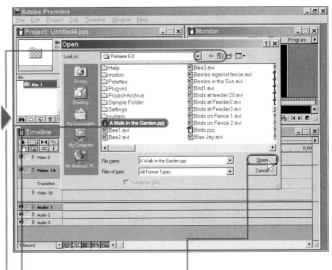

■1 Click **File**.

■2 Click **Open**.

■ The Open dialog box
appears.

*Note: To open a recently used
project file, click **File**, **Open Recent
Project**, and then the file.*

■3 Click the project file you
want to open.

■ You can click here to look
in other folders or drives.

■4 Click **Open**.

■ Premiere opens the
project file.

NAVIGATE PROJECT SETTINGS

You can choose from Premiere's project settings to determine program properties. Settings categories include: General, Video, Audio, Keyframe and Rendering, and Capture. You can set project settings when you start a new project, or you can fine-tune them when you prepare the project for output.

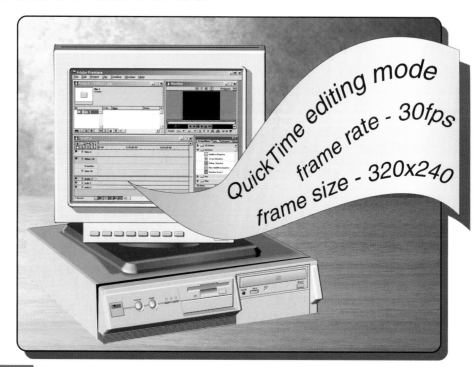

QuickTime editing mode
frame rate - 30fps
frame size - 320x240

NAVIGATE PROJECT SETTINGS

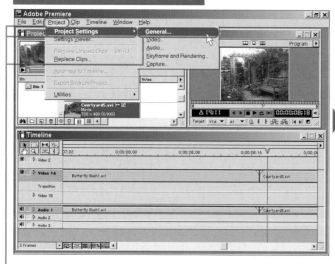

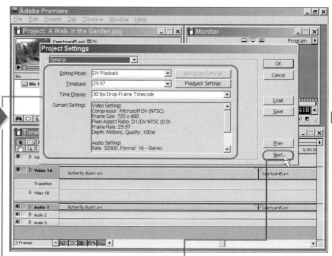

■1 Click **Project**.

■2 Click **Project Settings**.

■3 Click **General**.

Note: You can also access settings from the Load Project Settings dialog box when starting a new project. Click the Custom button.

■ The Project Settings dialog box appears and displays General settings.

Note: The settings you see in each of the project settings categories depend on your hardware setup.

■ You can make changes to the settings as needed.

■4 Click **Next**.

■ The Project Settings dialog box displays the Video settings.

30

How else can I view my project settings?

To view all of your project settings at once, open the Settings Viewer window. You can quickly see what settings have been applied for your project as well as settings for capture and export. You cannot, however, make changes to individual settings without returning to the Project Settings dialog box. See the section "Using the Settings Viewer" to learn more.

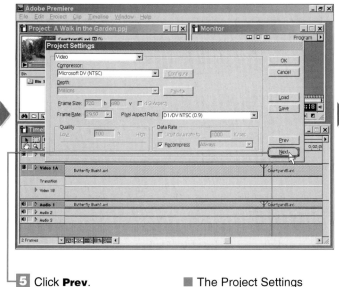

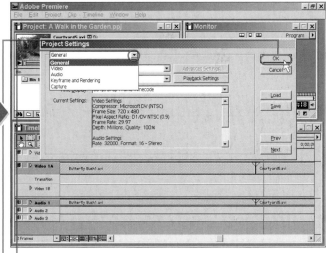

5 Click **Prev**.

■ The Project Settings dialog box returns to the General settings.

■ You can also click ▾ and then the category you want to view.

6 Click **OK**.

■ Premiere closes the Project Settings dialog box and applies any changes you made.

SAVE PROJECT SETTINGS

You can save any changes you make to the project settings and reuse the settings in another project. Premiere installs with a variety of presets for different hardware configurations and video needs, but you can customize these presets to suit your own work needs.

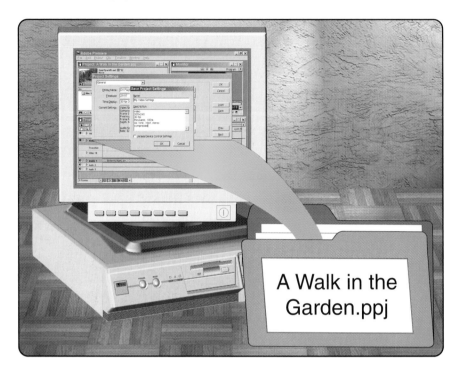

A Walk in the Garden.ppj

SAVE PROJECT SETTINGS

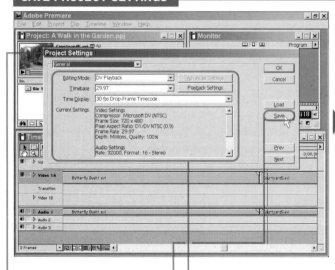

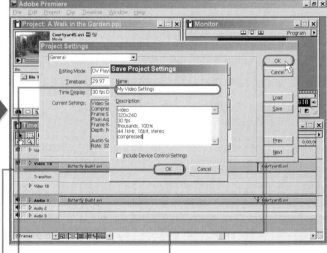

1 Open the Project Settings dialog box.

Note: See the section "Navigate Project Settings" to learn how to open the dialog box and view settings options.

2 Make the necessary changes to the settings categories.

3 Click **Save**.

■ The Save Project Settings dialog box appears.

4 Type a name for the file.

■ Optionally, you can type a description of the settings.

5 Click **OK**.

■ The settings are saved as a preset file.

6 Click **OK** again to close the Project Settings dialog box.

Note: See the section "Load Project Settings" to reuse the settings you saved.

LOAD PROJECT SETTINGS

You can load your project
settings and then use them
with another project.
Premiere stores project
settings files in the Settings
folder within the Premiere
program folder. Preset
project settings are listed in
the Load Project Settings
dialog box to allow you easy
access to them when you
begin a new project.

LOAD PROJECT SETTINGS

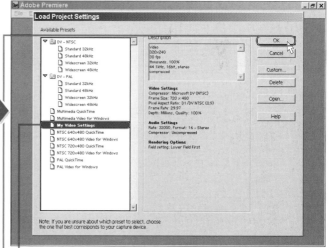

1 Start a new project or
launch Premiere.

*Note: See the section "Start a New
Project" to learn more.*

■ The Load Project Settings
dialog box appears.

2 Click the preset you want
to use.

3 Click **OK**.

■ A new project opens
using the presets you
selected.

*Note: See the section
"Understanding Premiere Settings"
to learn more about types of project
settings you can choose.*

USING THE SETTINGS VIEWER

You can view all the settings assigned to your project using Premiere's Settings Viewer window. The Settings Viewer lets you see settings for your project along with settings for capture and export.

USING THE SETTINGS VIEWER

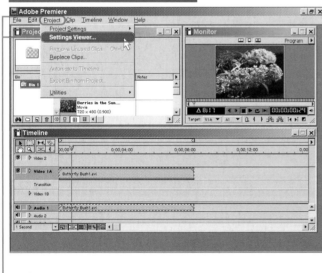

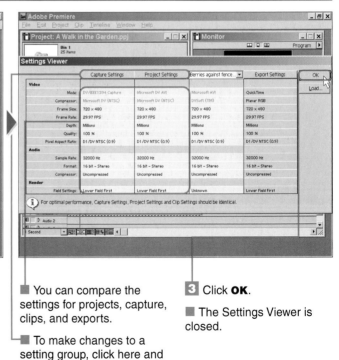

-1 Click **Project**.

-2 Click **Settings Viewer**.

■ The Settings Viewer window opens.

■ You can compare the settings for projects, capture, clips, and exports.

■ To make changes to a setting group, click here and the Project Settings dialog box appears.

3 Click **OK**.

■ The Settings Viewer is closed.

You can specify which
screen opens when you
start Premiere. By
default, the Load Project
Settings dialog box
appears. You can tell
Premiere to display the
Open dialog box, for
example, to quickly
access existing projects.

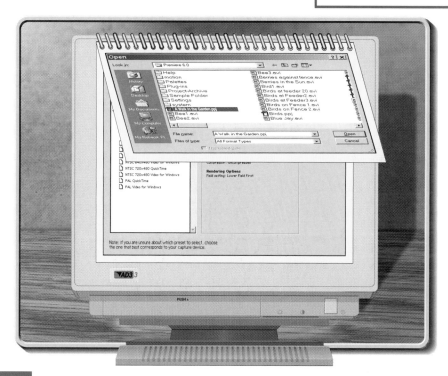

CHANGE THE STARTUP SCREEN

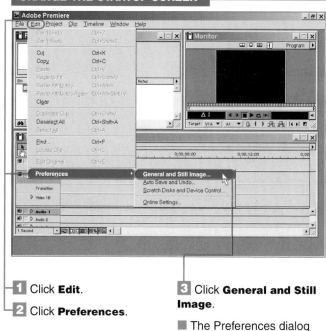

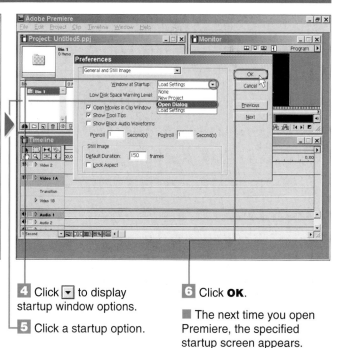

■1 Click **Edit**.

■2 Click **Preferences**.

■3 Click **General and Still Image**.

■ The Preferences dialog box appears.

■4 Click ▼ to display startup window options.

■5 Click a startup option.

■6 Click **OK**.

■ The next time you open Premiere, the specified startup screen appears.

You can use the Project window to manage the content of your video. The Project window lists all the clips and other production elements you plan to use in your project.

Preview Area

This area displays information about the selected clip or bin.

Project List

This area lists various production elements you want to use in your project.

Bin Area

This area displays the bins that are used to organize clips in your project.

Bin Icons

Click these buttons to control bins.

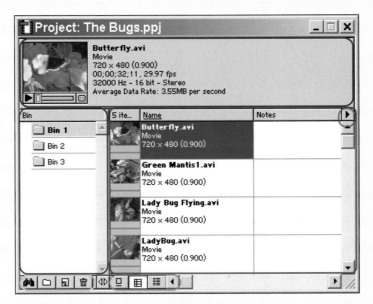

View Icons

Click these buttons to control how clips are listed in the Project window.

Project Window Menu

You can display a menu of commands pertaining to the Project window.

You can use the
Project window to
quickly view and
keep track of the
many source files
and clips you use
with your project.
The Project window
displays information
about each clip as
well as the bins
which organize
the clips.

CHANGE PROJECT WINDOW VIEWS

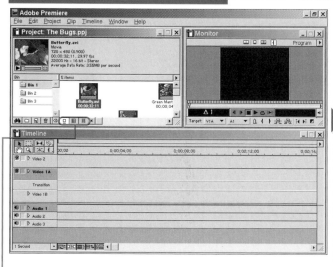 

1 Click a view icon.

■ Clicking 🖳 displays clips
as icons.

■ Clicking ⊞ displays clips
as thumbnail images along
with clip information.

■ Clicking ☰ displays clip
information in list format.

■ The Project window
changes the view format.

*Note: Thumbnail view is the default
view.*

CREATE A STORYBOARD

You can use a storyboard to help you put together a video project. Premiere's storyboard feature lets you arrange still images to represent the order in which you want the final video. You can save the arrangement as a storyboard file.

CREATE A STORYBOARD

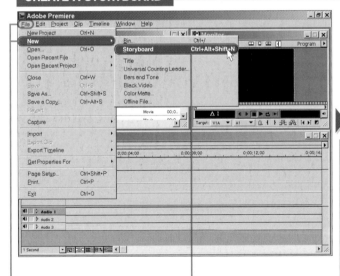

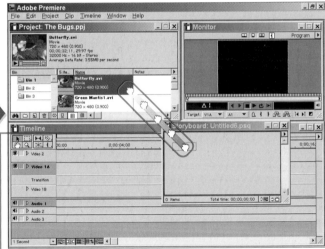

■1 Click **File**.

■2 Click **New**.

■3 Click **Storyboard**.

■ The Storyboard window opens.

■4 Click and drag the first clip you want to use from the Project window to the Storyboard window.

Note: If you have not yet imported clips, you can do so now. See Chapter 4 to import clips.

Can I create a storyboard in the Project window?

Yes. Place all the clips you want to use in the same bin, switch to icon view, and arrange the clips in the order you want to place them. To automate the clips to the timeline, click **Project**, **Automate to Timeline**. See the section "Change Project Window Views" to learn more about working in the Project window.

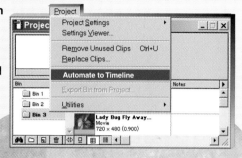

5 Continue dragging clips to assemble the video.

■ To reorder a clip in the Storyboard window, drag a clip to a new position.

■ You can resize the window by clicking and dragging its borders.

*Note: To add a note about the clip, double-click the note area, type the note text, and click **OK**.*

6 Click **File**.

7 Click **Save As**.

■ The Save File dialog box appears.

CONTINUED ▶ 39

CREATE A STORYBOARD

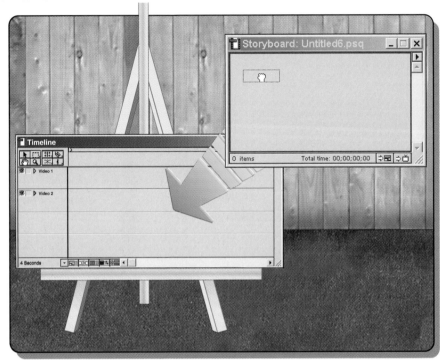

After creating your storyboard, you can tell Premiere to place the storyboard items into the Timeline window using the Automate to Timeline command.

CREATE A STORYBOARD (CONTINUED)

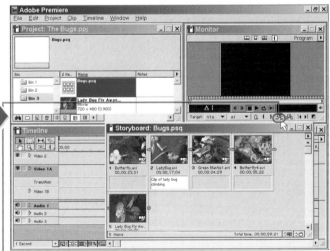

8 Type a name for the storyboard file.

9 Click **Save**.

■ Premiere saves the storyboard and adds it to the project window.

Note: Storyboard files are saved as PSQ file types.

10 Click the Automate to Timeline button (🔲).

■ The Automate to Timeline dialog box appears.

Can I edit a clip from the Storyboard window?

Yes. Double-click the clip's thumbnail image to open the Clip window. You can now edit the clip. See Chapters 5 and 7 to learn more about working with the Clip window and editing clips.

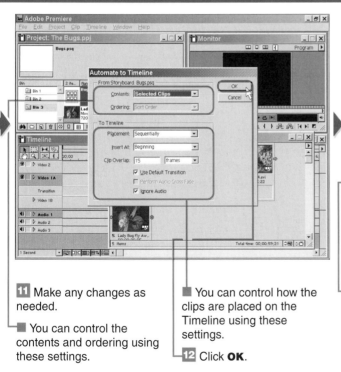

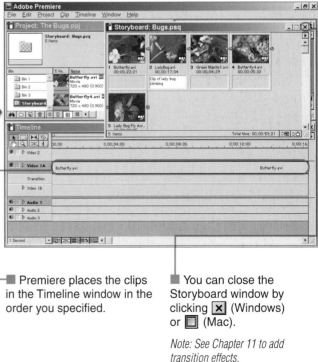

■ 11 Make any changes as needed.

■ You can control the contents and ordering using these settings.

■ You can control how the clips are placed on the Timeline using these settings.

■ 12 Click **OK**.

■ Premiere places the clips in the Timeline window in the order you specified.

■ You can close the Storyboard window by clicking ⊠ (Windows) or ▣ (Mac).

Note: See Chapter 11 to add transition effects.

CHAPTER 3

Capturing Video

Do you need to transfer video from your camcorder to Premiere? This chapter shows you how to capture video shot with a camcorder and add it to your Premiere project.

UNDERSTANDING VIDEO CAPTURE

You can transfer digital video directly from your DV camcorder to Premiere as long as you have the right connection hardware. The process, called *video capture*, sends data from one source to another.

Compression Basics

Digitized video is compressed regardless of what method of capture you use. To give you some idea of why compression is necessary, consider that every frame in an uncompressed digital video consumes up to 1 megabyte (MB) of space. The DV format compresses video at a 5:1 ratio.

Capture Limitations

Although the Premiere Timeline can hold up to three hours of video, your computer system and capture hardware impose file size limitations. Check the appropriate hardware documentation before capturing large amounts of video.

Digital Quality

The quality of the video you capture depends on the quality of the equipment you are using. Some digital camcorders may be able to produce higher-quality footage than others. Digital copies of the footage are clones of the original, but analog copies, such as those made from VHS tapes, degrade significantly in digital quality.

Capture Devices

Transferring sound and video from a DV camcorder to a computer requires an *IEEE-1394*, or *FireWire*, card or port on your computer as well as the same output ports on your camcorder. To capture video from analog sources, you need to use an analog to digital capture board. You must digitize any analog media if you want to use it in Premiere.

Device Control

If your camcorder and FireWire card are compatible with Premiere, you can use the device control built into Premiere to operate your camcorder or video deck from within the Premiere program window. Enabling device control lets you use the controls in the Movie Capture window to play, stop, and rewind the tape.

Timecode

Videotape uses an encoded signal called a *timecode* to identify each frame of the captured video. The timecode number includes hours, minutes, seconds, and frames. Premiere can use timecode to assist with capturing clips, particularly with capturing a batch of clips.

Batch Capture

If you are using device control and time-coded tape, you can capture batches of clips automatically. Premiere locates each clip you specify in a batch list and captures the clip for you.

You can use the Movie Capture window to transfer video from a digital camcorder to your Premiere project. You can preview your video before recording it to a clip, cue the video to the segment you want to record, or set up capture settings.

WORK WITH THE MOVIE CAPTURE WINDOW

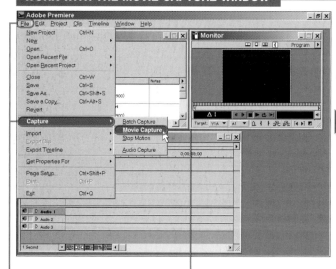

1 With a Premiere project open, click **File**.

2 Click **Capture**.

3 Click **Movie Capture**.

■ The Movie Capture window opens.

■ You can view the video in the Preview area.

■ Use these buttons to control playback of the video.

■ If device control is enabled, you can also use these controls to control your camcorder or DV device.

■ The video's timecode appears here.

How do I capture video from a VHS camcorder or VCR?

You must convert analog VHS, VHS-C, or Video-8 signals to digital with a capture card in your computer or other conversion device. Refer to the hardware documentation for details about configuring and using those devices.

■ These icons toggle video and audio capture on or off when not using device control.

■ On the Settings tab, you can view and specify capture settings and preferences.

■ Clicking here displays the Movie Capture window menu.

■ Clicking the **Logging** tab lets you log clips for batch capture.

■ To close the Movie Capture window when finished, click ⊠ (Windows) or ▣ (Mac).

CHANGE CAPTURE SETTINGS

You can change capture settings using the Project Settings dialog box. The options available to you depend on the equipment you are using. For example, users whose computers have IEEE 1394/FireWire ports have different options than those with capture boards installed.

CHANGE CAPTURE SETTINGS

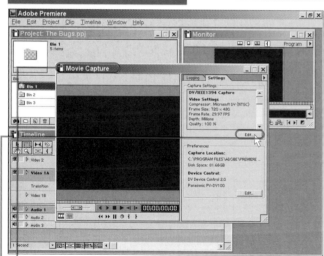

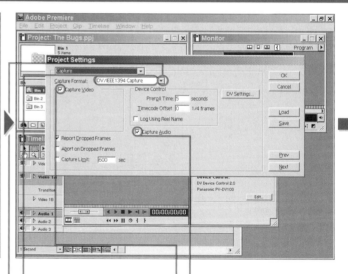

1 With a Premiere project open, open the Movie Capture window.

Note: See the section "Work with the Movie Capture Window" to open the window.

2 Click the **Edit** button.

■ The Project Settings dialog box appears and displays Capture settings.

*Note: If the Capture settings are not displayed, click the **Next** or **Prev** buttons to navigate to the options.*

3 Change any capture settings as needed.

Note: The options available are based on your hardware and system setup.

■ To change capture format, click here.

■ To capture audio without video, click this option (☐ changes to ☑).

■ To capture video without audio, click this option (☐ changes to ☑).

What do the Device Control settings do?

If device control is enabled, the Capture category's options are enabled; if not, the options are dimmed. The options enable you to control the playing of the source tape in a DV device, such as a DV camcorder. For example, you can set the Preroll Time option to specify how many seconds of tape rewind to get up to speed for capture.

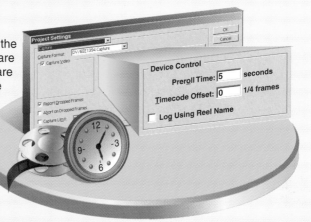

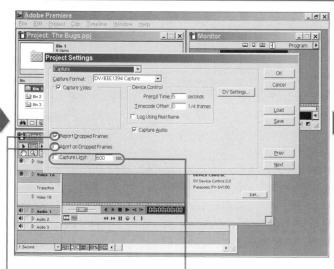

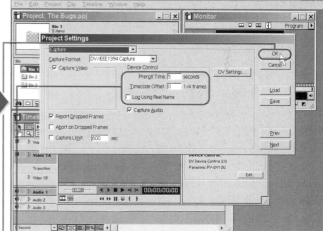

■ Click this option to keep track of dropped frames that occur during capture (☐ changes to ☑).

■ If you want to stop the capture if frames are dropped, click this option (☐ changes to ☑).

■ Click this option to set a time limit, in seconds, for the capture (☐ changes to ☑).

■ If using device control, you can set Device Control options.

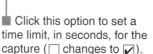 Click **OK**.

■ The Project Settings dialog box closes and any new settings take effect.

SET THE SCRATCH DISK

You can control where your captured videos are stored and processed by designating a *scratch disk.* It is a good idea to use your fastest hard drive for video capture. If you are using your computer's hard drive, you should also defragment and optimize the hard drive first. You can specify a scratch disk for capture using the Movie Capture window.

SET THE SCRATCH DISK

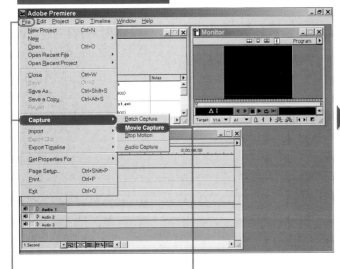

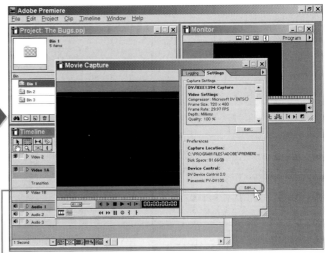

 **1** Click **File**.

2 Click **Capture**.

3 Click **Movie Capture**.

■ The Movie Capture window appears.

4 Under the Preferences heading in the Settings tab, click the **Edit** button.

■ The Preferences dialog box appears and displays the Scratch Disks and Device Control options.

What exactly is a scratch disk?

As you edit digital video, changes are processed in your computer's RAM. If RAM is exceeded, your hard drive can serve as another work area. Premiere uses a designated scratch disk like a paper scratch pad to handle overflow files created while editing, such as previewing files and capturing clips.

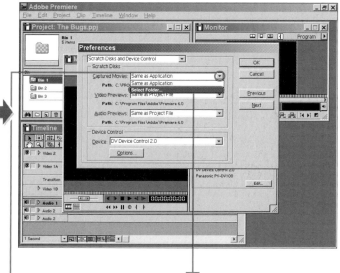

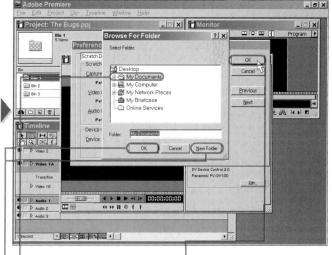

*Note: If the Scratch Disks and Device Control settings do not appear, click the **Next** or **Prev** buttons to navigate to the options.*

5 Click the **Captured Movies** ▼.

6 Click **Select Folder**.

*Note: Click **Same As Application** if you want to use the hard disk drive where Premiere is stored.*

■ The Browse For Folder dialog box appears.

7 Select a folder.

■ To create a new folder, click here and then type a folder name.

8 Click **OK**.

9 Click **OK** again to exit the Preferences dialog box.

■ Any clips you capture now are saved to the folder and scratch disk you specified.

You can use the Movie Capture window to capture video footage directly into your project. With device control activated, you can control your camcorder from within the Premiere program window.

CAPTURE VIDEO IN THE CAPTURE WINDOW

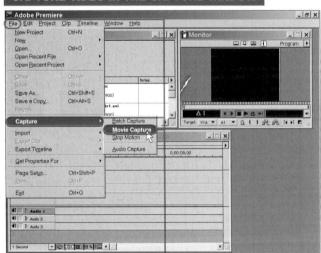

1 Turn on your camcorder and set it to VCR/VTR mode.

Note: See the section "Understanding Video Capture" to learn more about required hardware.

2 Open the project and bin to which you want to capture.

Note: See Chapter 2 to open a project.

3 Click **File**.

4 Click **Capture**.

5 Click **Movie Capture**.

■ The Movie Capture window opens.

6 Cue the video to the scene you want to capture.

■ Device control allows you to use the controls on either the camcorder or the Movie Capture window to cue the video.

7 Click the Play button (▶).

■ If you are not using device control, click ▶ on the camcorder.

8 Click the Record button (⦿).

■ Premiere starts transferring the footage.

How do I enable device control?

Turn on your DV device and start Premiere. In the Movie Capture window, follow these steps:

1 Click the **Edit** button on the Settings tab under the Preferences heading.

2 Click the **Device** ⏷ located in the Scratch Disks & Device Control category.

3 Click the device controller you are using.

To set additional options for the device, click the **Options** button. If Premiere does not recognize your camcorder, be sure to check www.adobe.com and their DV hardware compatibility database for more information.

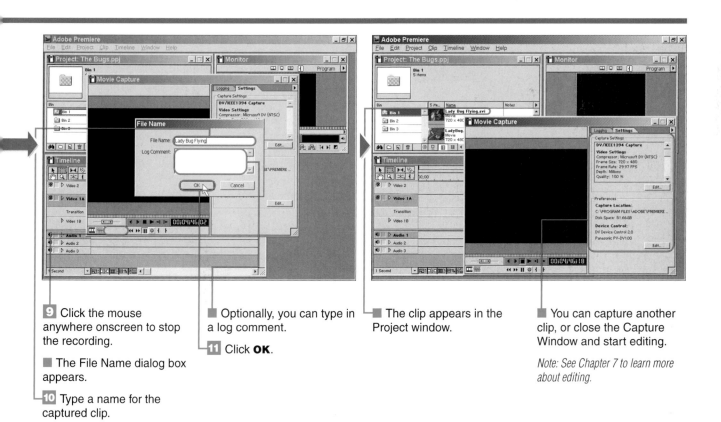

9 Click the mouse anywhere onscreen to stop the recording.

■ The File Name dialog box appears.

10 Type a name for the captured clip.

■ Optionally, you can type in a log comment.

11 Click **OK**.

■ The clip appears in the Project window.

■ You can capture another clip, or close the Capture Window and start editing.

Note: See Chapter 7 to learn more about editing.

PERFORM A BATCH CAPTURE

You can automate the capture process by performing a batch capture. If you are using device control and time-coded tape, you can batch capture clips into Premiere. Start by making a list of the segments you want to capture, and then tell Premiere to capture each clip in the list. A batch list is saved as a special batch list file type and can be reopened and edited as needed.

PERFORM A BATCH CAPTURE

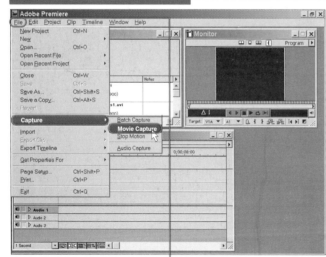

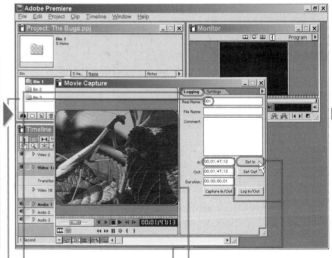

CREATE A CAPTURE LIST

■1 Connect and turn on the DV device or hardware you want to use for capturing.

Note: See the section "Understanding Video Capture" to learn more about required hardware.

■2 Click **File**.

■3 Click **Capture**.

■4 Click **Movie Capture**.

■ The Movie Capture window opens.

■5 Click the **Logging** tab.

■ The Logging tab displays options for batch lists.

■6 Type the name of the reel or tape you are using.

■7 Cue the tape to the frame you want to start from for the first clip you want to capture.

■8 Click the **Set In** button.

■ The current timecode is listed here.

How do I create a batch list if I am not using device control?

Click **File**, **Capture**, and then **Batch Control** to open an untitled Batch Capture window. Click 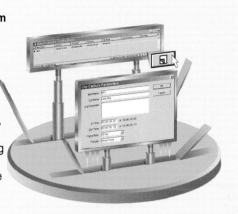 to open the Clip Capture Parameters window, where you can specify reel name, clip name, and timecode in and out points. After manually entering information about the clip, click **OK** to send the information to the Batch Capture window. You can save the list and batch capture when you are ready.

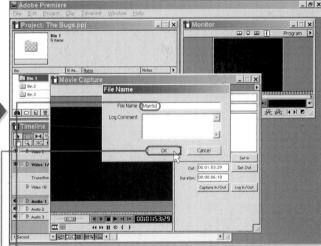

9 Cue the tape to the frame where you want to stop the capture.

10 Click the **Set Out** button.

■ The current timecode is listed here.

11 Click the **Log In/Out** button.

■ The File Name dialog box appears.

12 Type a name for the captured clip.

13 Click **OK**.

■ The clip appears in the batch list.

Note: The Batch Capture window appears onscreen after you create the first clip in the list.

14 Continue adding clips to your batch list by following steps **7** through **13**.

■ Each clip you log is added to the batch list.

CONTINUED ▶ **55**

PERFORM A BATCH CAPTURE

After assembling a batch list, you can start capturing the clips listed. The icons that appear next to the clips in a batch list can help tell you about the clip's capture status. Before you begin the capturing process, be sure to make the necessary hardware connections and change any settings, such as the designated scratch disk.

SPORTS CAR
SPHINX
EXOTIC FISH
SEA SCAPE
BRIDGE

PERFORM A BATCH CAPTURE (CONTINUED)

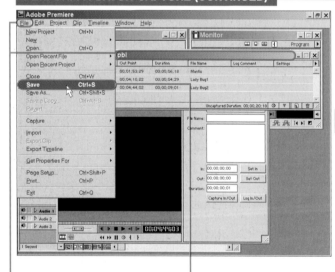

15 Click the batch list window's title bar.

16 Click **File**.

17 Click **Save**.

■ The Save File dialog box appears.

18 Type a filename for the list.

■ Batch lists are saves as PBL file types.

Note: Mac users should add the .pbl extension to the filename to keep the list cross-platform compatible.

19 Click **Save**.

■ The batch list is saved.

■ You can close the batch list window and the Movie Capture window and capture the clips when ready.

Why did Premiere abort my batch capture?

If your tape has unrecorded areas or gaps, the broken timecode sequence can cause Premiere to abort the batch capture. To work around the problem, you can log clips manually by entering in and out times. To avoid timecode gaps in the future, make sure you fully understand how your camcorder records, particularly when starting and stopping scenes.

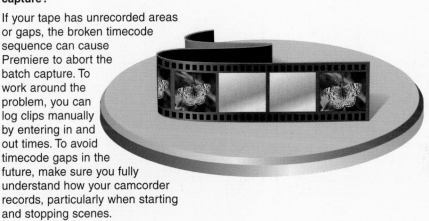

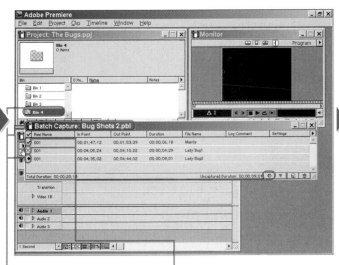

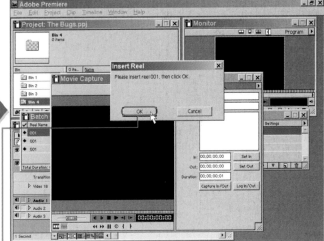

CAPTURE THE LISTED CLIPS

1 Click a bin in which to store the batch captured clips.

2 Open the batch list.

■ A ◆ icon indicates the clip will be captured.

■ A ✓ icon indicates the clip has been captured.

■ A ✕ icon indicates an error during capture.

3 Click the Record button (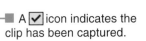).

■ Premiere prompts you to insert the reel or tape.

Note: Premiere saves clips to the scratch disk that you already set. See "Set the Scratch Disk" to learn more.

4 Click **OK**.

■ The Movie Capture window captures the clips.

*Note: To save the current status of a batch list, click **File**, then **Save** while the batch list window is active.*

ADD TIMECODE TO A CLIP

You can add timecode to a clip to help you accurately read frames for editing. Many DV camcorders can record timecode, and if you use device control when capturing video, the timecode is captured along with the clip. In some instances, the timecode appears on a separate track called a *window dub*. You can mark the timecode on your captured video manually.

APPLYING TIMECODE

00;01;46;24

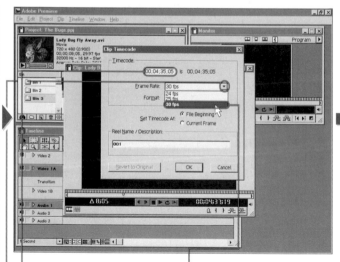

1 Open the clip to which you want to assign timecode.

Note: See Chapter 5 to work with clips.

2 Click **Clip**.

3 Click **Advanced Options**.

4 Click **Timecode**.

■ The Clip Timecode dialog box appears.

5 Type the timecode number that matches the current frame.

6 Click ▼ to display available frame rates.

7 Click a frame rate that matches the source video.

Is timecode a part of all videotapes?

Timecode is added to tapes you record to using device control. Timecode is recorded on a track that is separate from the video and audio tracks on a tape. The process is called *striping*. Home VCRs, for example, do not add timecode to the tape.

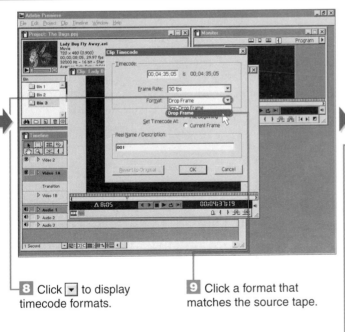

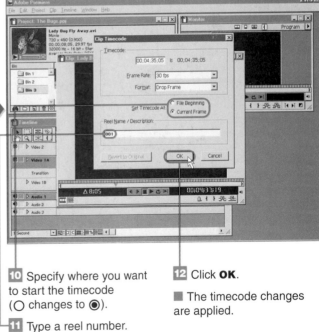

8 Click ▼ to display timecode formats.

9 Click a format that matches the source tape.

10 Specify where you want to start the timecode (○ changes to ◉).

11 Type a reel number.

12 Click **OK**.

■ The timecode changes are applied.

CHAPTER 4

Importing Production Elements

Are you ready to start creating your project? This chapter shows you how to add production elements, such as video and audio clips, to your project.

UNDERSTANDING PRODUCTION ELEMENTS

When you have set up your Premiere project file, you are ready to start adding *content*. Content includes the various production elements that go into the making of your project, such as video files, graphics files, still images, and audio files.

Digital Media

Production elements you import into Premiere must be in digital format. *Digital media* is content represented by 1's and 0's that can be read and manipulated by a computer. Digital media equipment is fast becoming a popular way to capture video today.

Analog Media

Prior to digital media equipment, video content was generally analog in format. Motion picture film and audiocassette tape are two examples. You cannot use analog media in Premiere without first converting the media to digital form by digitizing it. To convert analog video to digital, see Chapter 3.

Clips

The content you add to a project file is referred to as *clips*. You can import as many clips as you need to help you complete your project. Premiere lists clips in bins in the Project window.

Video Clips

Premiere supports the two most popular digital video file formats, QuickTime and AVI, as well as other video file formats.

Audio Clips

Premiere supports AIFF and WAV sound files and lets you import sounds from video tracks. Premiere does not support Compact Disc Audio (CDA) format.

Still Images

You can also import graphics files or still images, such as photographs (raster images) and drawings (vector images) created in other programs, into your Premiere projects.

Animation Sequences

When you import a sequence of still images, Premiere treats the group of images as a single clip. For example, you may import an animation, which consists of a series or sequential images.

IMPORT A CLIP

You can import video and audio clips into your Premiere project from other sources. Premiere also imports still images, including TIFF and JPEG graphic files. Premiere enables you to import either one clip or many, which appear in the Project window.

Clips cannot exceed 4,000 x 4,000 pixels in size.

IMPORT A SINGLE CLIP

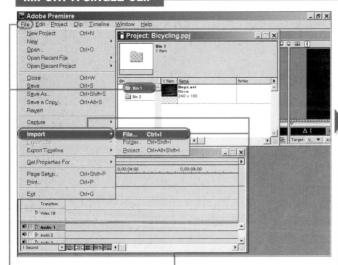

1 Click the bin to which you want to import.

Note: See the section "Organize Clips" to learn more about working with bins.

2 Click **File**.

3 Click **Import**.

4 Click **File**.

■ The Import dialog box opens.

5 Click the file you want to import.

■ You can click the Look in ▼ to navigate to a particular file or folder.

6 Click **Open**.

■ You can also double-click the filename to quickly import the file.

■ The file is imported and appears listed in the Project window.

Note: See Chapter 2 to learn more about the Project window.

64

Why does Premiere call them bins and clips rather than files and folders?

The terms *bins* and *clips* are taken from the world of motion picture film editing. Editors used to clip a section of processed film to a wire and allow it to fall into a cotton lined trash bin or basket. Any sections of the filmstrip that had to be cut out, or *clipped*, were hung in the bin until the editor was ready to cement them into place on the filmstrip.

IMPORT MULTIPLE CLIPS

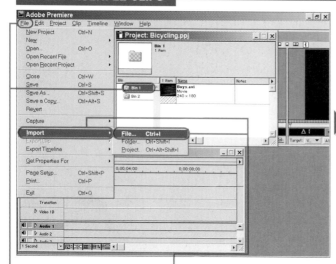

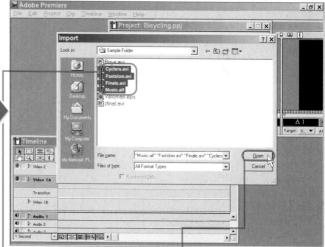

1 Click the bin to which you want to import.

Note: See the section "Organize Clips" to learn more about working with bins.

2 Click **File**.

3 Click **Import**.

4 Click **File**.

■ The Import dialog box opens.

■ You can click the Look in ▾ to navigate to a particular file or folder.

5 Press **Ctrl** (Windows) or **Shift** (Mac).

6 Click each filename you want to import.

7 Click **Open**.

■ The files are imported and listed in the Project window.

Note: See Chapter 6 to learn more about working with clips in the Project window.

ORGANIZE CLIPS

You can organize imported clips in the Premiere Project window. You can create new bins to hold clips and move the clips from one bin to another.

A bin is simply a subfolder in your project where you can store production elements.

CREATE A NEW BIN

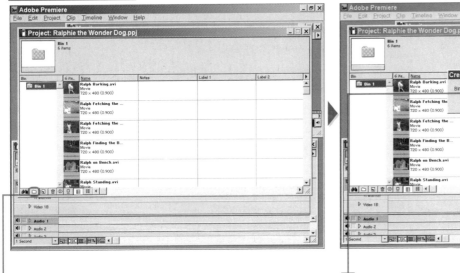

1 Click **New Bin** button (⬜).

Note: See Chapter 2 to learn more about working with the Project window.

■ The Create Bin dialog box opens.

2 Type a name for the new bin.

3 Click **OK**.

■ The new bin appears listed in the Project window.

Can I rename a bin?

Yes. You can rename a bin at
any time to help you better
organize your project. To
rename a bin, follow these
steps:

1 Double-click the bin name.

2 Type a new name.

3 Press `Enter`.

4 The bin is
renamed. See
Chapter 6 to rename clips.

MOVE A CLIP TO ANOTHER BIN

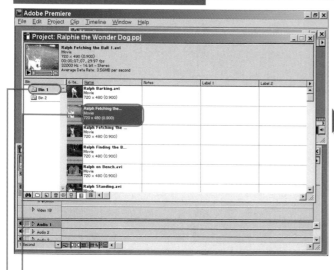

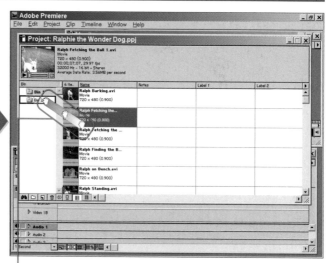

1 Click the bin containing
the clip you want to move.

2 Click the clip you want
to move.

■ To move multiple clips,
hold down the `Shift` or
`Control` key while clicking
clips.

3 Click and drag the clip to
another bin.

4 Release the mouse
button.

■ The clip is moved.

SET A FRAME DURATION FOR IMPORTED STILL IMAGES

You can import a still image or graphic file into your project to play for a designated number of frames, even though the image itself comprises only a single frame. Set the frame duration in Premiere before importing the image file into your project.

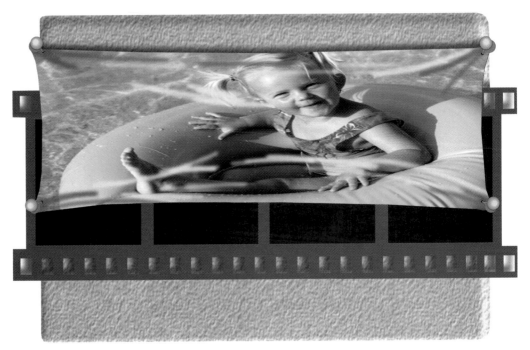

SET A FRAME DURATION FOR IMPORTED STILL IMAGES

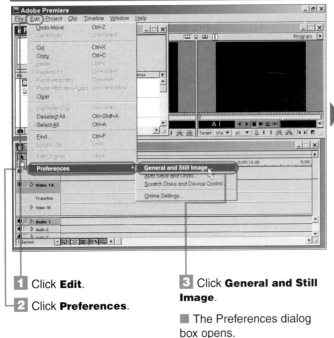

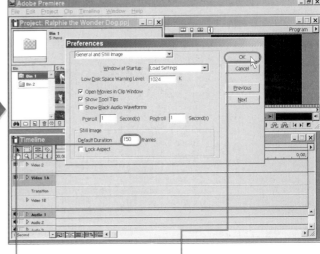

1 Click **Edit**.

2 Click **Preferences**.

3 Click **General and Still Image**.

■ The Preferences dialog box opens.

4 Type the number of frames you want to apply to imported still images.

Note: Still images previously imported are not affected by the new setting you type.

5 Click **OK**.

■ Any new still images you import will use the frame duration specified.

Note: See the section "Import a Clip" to import image files.

LOCK THE ASPECT RATIO FOR IMPORTED STILL IMAGES

By default, Premiere automatically sizes imported still images to fit the video frame size. If the image requires a different sizing ratio, you can lock the image's ratio before importing the image into Premiere.

If the image's aspect ratio differs from your project's settings, the image may appear with borders.

LOCK THE ASPECT RATIO FOR IMPORTED STILL IMAGES

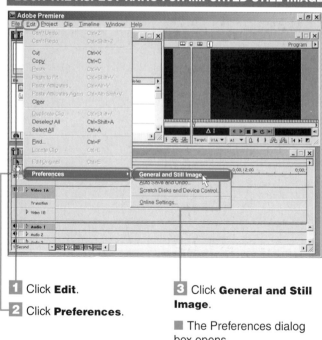

1 Click **Edit**.

2 Click **Preferences**.

3 Click **General and Still Image**.

■ The Preferences dialog box opens.

4 To keep the image's aspect ratio, click Lock Aspect (☐ changes to ✔).

5 Click **OK**.

■ The next still image you import keeps its original aspect ratio.

Note: See the section "Import a Clip" to import image files.

IMPORT STILL IMAGE SEQUENCES

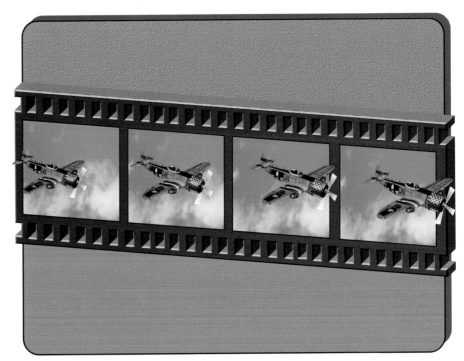

You can import a sequence of still images into Premiere and treat it as a single clip. Some programs export movies in this manner. As long as the images use a numbering convention, Premiere treats each numbered image as a frame in the movie.

IMPORT STILL IMAGE SEQUENCES

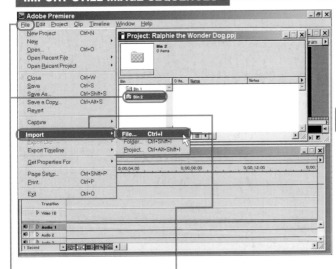

1 Click the bin to which you want to import.

Note: See the section "Organize Clips" to learn more about working with bins.

2 Click **File**.

3 Click **Import**.

4 Click **File**.

■ The Import dialog box opens.

5 Click the first file in the sequence you want to import.

■ *You can click the Look in* ▼ *to navigate to a particular file or folder.*

I tried to import a sequence of images, but the resulting clip is not correct. What went wrong?

Make sure that each image in the sequence uses an equal number of digits in the filename, and uses the same file extensions, such as image001, image002, and so on. Also make sure that you click the very first still image in the sequence when selecting the sequence in the Import dialog box.

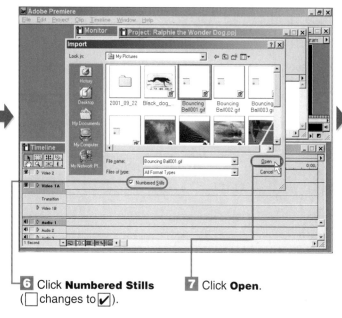

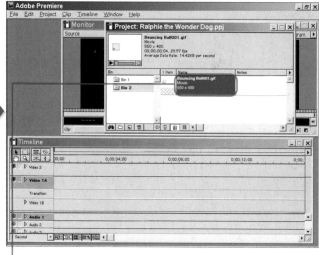

6 Click **Numbered Stills** (☐ changes to ☑).

7 Click **Open**.

■ The sequence is imported and appears listed as a single clip in the Project window.

Note: See Chapter 6 to learn more about working with clips in the Project window.

IMPORT A PROJECT

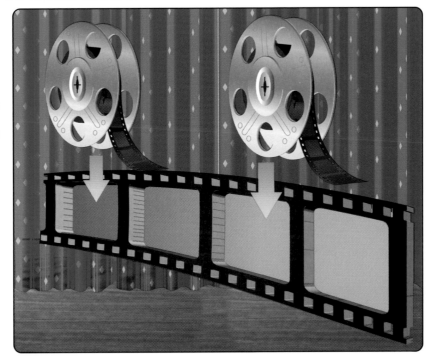

You can import one project into another to create a larger project. For example, you may want to create separate project files for portions of your video, and then combine them into one project file to create the final movie.

You can open only one project at a time with Premiere.

IMPORT A PROJECT

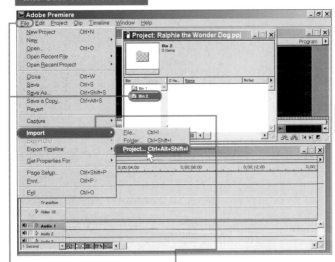

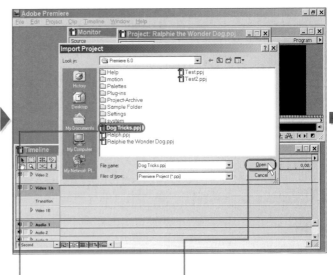

■1 Click the bin to which you want to import.

Note: See the section "Organize Clips" to learn more about working with bins.

■2 Click **File**.

■3 Click **Import**.

■4 Click **Project**.

■ The Import Project dialog box opens.

■5 Click the project file you want to import.

■ You can click the Look in ▼ to navigate to a particular file or folder.

■6 Click **Open**.

■ A smaller Import Project dialog box opens.

Can I import Premiere 5.0 projects into Premiere 6.0 projects?

No. You must first save the Premiere 5.0 project as a Premiere 6.0 file; then, you can import it into your project file. Simply open the Premiere 5.0 project in Premiere 6.0 and save it as a 6.0 project file.

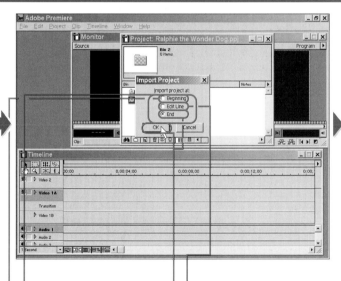

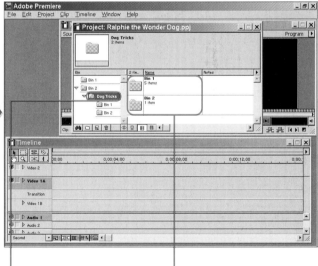

7 Click an option to specify where the imported project begins within the existing project.

■ Click this option to start the imported project at the beginning of the current project.

■ Clicking this option lets you insert the project at the edit line of the current project.

■ You can click this option to insert the project at the end of the current project.

8 Click **OK**.

■ The project is imported.

■ Associated clips are listed in a bin of the same name.

ADDING TITLE TEXT

...OPENING PROJECT CLIP...

CHAPTER 5

Working with Clips

Are you ready to start working with your clips? Whether you import or capture clips, this chapter shows you how to work with clips in Premiere.

UNDERSTANDING CLIPS

Your video project is based on *clips*. Clips are production elements you use to assemble your video. For example, in an action video you may have a clip showing a man driving up to a building and another clip showing the same man entering the building. Yet another clip may show a close-up of the man's face. By putting the clips together, you create a scene.

Where Do I Find Clips?

Clips can be created from digital video footage shot with a camcorder, or from digital clips stored on your computer. To learn how to transfer video from a camcorder into Premiere, see Chapter 3. To learn more about importing clips into Premiere, see Chapter 4. Regardless of the source of your footage, all clips you use in Premiere must be digitized.

What Kinds of Clips Can I Use?

Digital video is the main type of clip you will work with in Premiere. You can also use static clips, such as graphics, photographs, or text, for example. You can create title clips and simple graphics in Premiere using the Title window. See Chapter 12 to learn more about the titling feature.

Viewing Clips

You can use several different methods to view a clip in Premiere. You can open the clip in a separate Clip window that has control for playing the clip, or you can play a clip directly in the Project window. You can use the Source view area in the Monitor window to view and edit a clip. To add a clip to the project, you must add the clip to the project's timeline. After you add clips to the Timeline window, you can view the video using the Program view area of the Monitor window.

Editing Clips

Premiere offers several routes that you can take to edit the clips you want to use in your video. You can perform a few editing techniques within the Clip window, but most of your editing, however, occurs in either the Monitor or Timeline windows, or a combination of both. To learn more about editing in either window, see Chapters 7 and 8.

Setting In and Out Points

An important editing technique to master is trimming the clip by setting in and out points. The *in point* is the frame in which the clip starts. The *out point* is the frame in which the clip ends. By setting in and out points, you determine the length of the clip. You can set in and out points in the Clip window as well as the Monitor and Timeline windows.

Adding Clips to the Timeline

To use a clip in your video, you must add it to the Timeline window. Video, still image, and title clips appear in the timeline's video tracks. Sound clips appear in the timeline's audio tracks. To learn more about using the Timeline window, see Chapter 6.

VIEW A VIDEO CLIP

You can open a video clip and view it in the Clip window. The Clip window includes controls for playing, stopping, looping, and editing the clip. The Clip window for still image clips does not feature playback controls.

See the section "View a Still Image Clip" to learn more about viewing still images.

VIEW A VIDEO CLIP

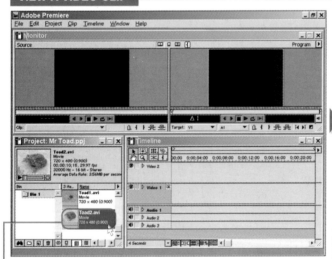

1 With a project open, double-click the clip you want to view.

Note: See Chapter 3 to capture video, and see Chapter 4 to import clips.

■ The Clip window opens.

2 Click ▶.

■ The clip plays.

■ You can click and drag the **Set Location** marker (▽) to a particular point in the clip to play.

■ Clicking ■ stops the clip from playing.

■ Clicking ↻ plays the clip continually.

■ Clicking ◀ and ▶ moves the Set Location marker back or forward a frame.

3 Click ✕ (Windows) or ☐ (Mac) to close the Clip window.

PLAY A SOUND CLIP

You can open an audio clip in the Clip window to see a waveform representation of the sound and hear the sound play. The Clip window includes controls for playing, stopping, looping, and editing the sound clip.

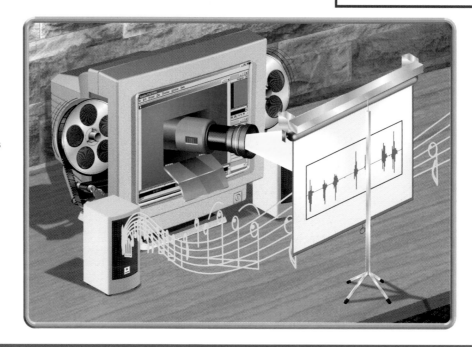

PLAY A SOUND CLIP

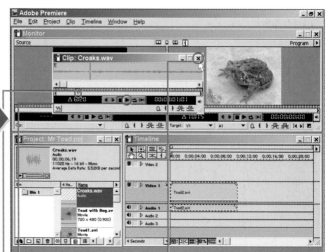

■1 With a project open, double-click the sound clip.

■ The Clip window opens.

Note: See Chapter 3 to capture video, and see Chapter 4 to import clips.

■2 Click ▶.

■ The clip plays.

■ You can click the **Set Location** marker (▽) to a particular point in the clip to play.

■ Clicking ■ stops the clip from playing.

■ Clicking 🔁 plays the clip continually.

■ Clicking 〽 cycles through various views of the waveform.

■3 Click ⊠ (Windows) or ▣ (Mac) to close the Clip window.

VIEW A STILL IMAGE CLIP

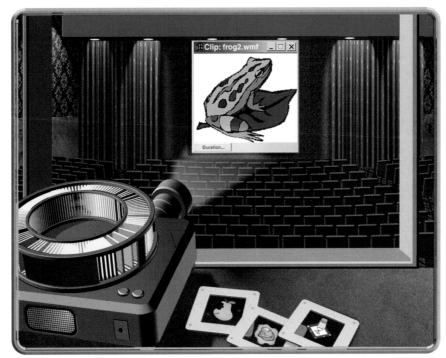

You can open a still image clip, such as a graphic, and view it in the Clip window. The Clip window for still image clips does not provide playback controls because still images consume only one video frame. However, you can set the duration of a still image to play for any number of frames.

VIEW A STILL IMAGE CLIP

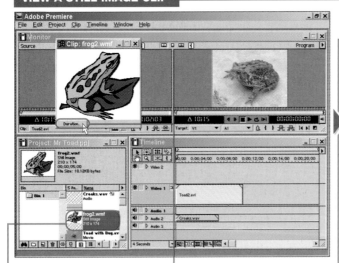

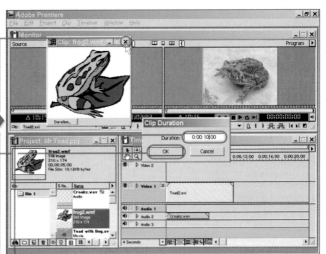

1 With a project open, double-click the clip you want to view.

Note: See Chapter 3 to capture video, and see Chapter 4 to import clips.

■ The Clip window opens.

2 Click the **Duration** button.

■ The Clip Duration dialog box appears.

3 Type the number of frames you want the still image to play.

4 Click **OK**.

5 Click ☒ (Windows) or ▣ (Mac) to close the Clip window.

■ When you add it to the Timeline, the clip plays for the designated number of frames.

Note: See Chapter 8 to add clips to the Timeline.

RENAME A CLIP

You can give clips *alias names* to help you identify them. When you import a clip, the project file references the clip's original location, but the clip itself is not saved until you export the video. For that reason, you should not rename a clip, but rather create an alias name.

The alias name does not affect the original clip name or reference.

RENAME A CLIP

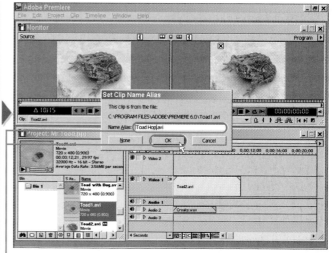

1 Click the clip to which you want to assign an alias name.

Note: See Chapter 3 to capture video, and see Chapter 4 to import clips.

2 Click **Clip**.

3 Click **Set Clip Name Alias**.

■ The Set Clip Name Alias dialog box appears.

4 Type a name for the clip.

5 Click **OK**.

■ The clip now uses the alias name in Premiere.

SET IN AND OUT POINTS FOR A VIDEO CLIP

You can set a clip's in and out points in the Clip window to ensure that you use only the footage you want in the video. The in point determines where the clip starts. The out point determines where the clip ends.

SET IN AND OUT POINTS FOR A VIDEO CLIP

1 With a project open, double-click the clip you want to edit.

Note: See Chapter 3 to capture video and see Chapter 4 to import clips.

■ The Clip window opens.

2 Click and drag the **Set Location** marker (▽) to the frame you want to set as the in point.

Note: See "View a Video Clip" to play a clip to determine edit points.

3 Click the **Mark In** button (⬚).

■ An in point icon ({) appears at the current frame.

■ The time readout shows the frame number.

How do I resize the Clip window?

Move the mouse pointer over the lower-right corner of the window, and then click and drag the edge to create a new window size.

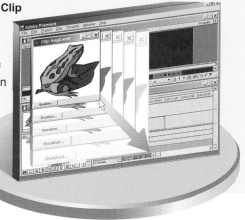

4 Click and drag the **Set Location** marker (▽) to the frame you want to set as the out point.

Note: See "View a Video Clip" to play a clip to determine edit points.

5 Click the **Mark Out** button ([↑]).

■ An out point icon (↑) appears at the current frame.

■ The time readout shows the frame number.

6 Click the **Play In to Out** button ([▶]) to play the clip.

■ Dragging in and out point adjusts their locations.

■ Clip duration displays here.

7 Click ☒ (Windows) or ▢ (Mac) to close the Clip window.

■ You can now add the clip to the Timeline.

Note: See Chapter 8 to add clips to the Timeline window.

SET IN AND OUT POINTS FOR AN AUDIO CLIP

You can set in and out points for sound clips using the Clip window. Setting in and out points lets you trim the sound to the length you want. The in point determines where the sound starts. The out point determines where the sound ends.

SET IN AND OUT POINTS FOR AN AUDIO CLIP

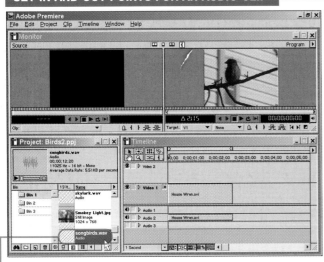

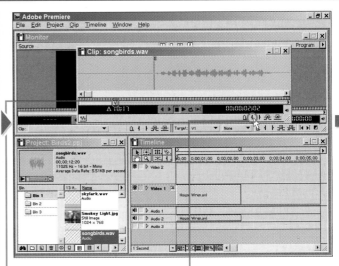

1 With a project open, double-click the clip you want to edit.

Note: See Chapter 3 to capture video, and see Chapter 4 to import clips.

■ The Clip window opens.

2 Click and drag the **Set Location** marker (▽) to the frame you want to set as the in point.

Note: See "View a Video Clip" to play a clip to determine edit points.

3 Click the **Mark In** button (▮).

■ An in point icon (▮) appears at the current frame.

How can I trim an audio clip that was captured with the video footage?

Premiere treats audio that was recorded with a video as a linked clip. If you try to set in and out points for the audio clip, the points are set for the linked video clip as well. To edit the audio separately, you must unlink the two clips. See Chapter 8 to learn how to unlink the two files.

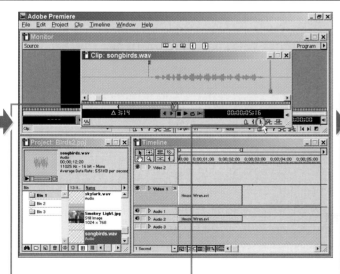

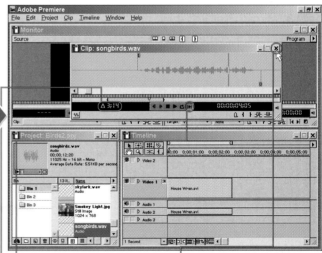

4 Click and drag the **Set Location** marker (▽) to the frame you want to set as the out point.

Note: See "View a Video Clip" to play a clip to determine edit points.

5 Click the **Mark Out** button (▮▸).

■ An out point icon (▸) appears at the current frame.

6 Click the **Play In to Out** button (▮▶) to play the clip.

■ Click ◀ and ▶ to adjust the clip, if needed.

■ The clip's duration appears here.

7 Click ✕ (Windows) or ▢ (Mac) to close the Clip window.

■ You can now add the clip to the Timeline.

Note: See Chapter 8 to add clips to the Timeline window.

ADD A LEADER CLIP

You can use Premiere source files to create *leader clips*. A leader clip appears at the beginning of a video showing a color bar and tone or a countdown that starts before the start of the actual video. You need leader clips if you plan to send your project to a production house to be finished.

ADD A LEADER CLIP

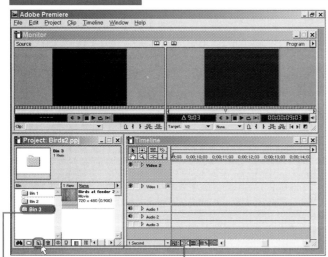

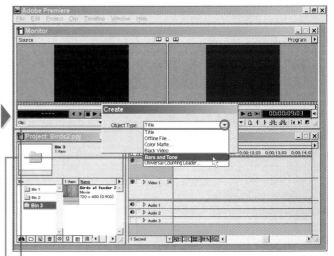

ADD A BARS AND TONE CLIP

1 Click on the bin in which you want to store a leader clip.

Note: See Chapter 4 to organize clips.

2 Click the **Create Item** button (![icon]).

■ The Create dialog box appears.

3 Click ![arrow] to display object types.

4 Click **Bars and Tone**.

5 Click **OK**.

■ Premiere adds a Bars and Tone clip to the Project window.

■ You can add the clip to your project at any time.

Note: See Chapter 8 to add a clip to the Timeline.

**How do I create plain black
footage for a leader clip?**

Click the **Create Item** button
(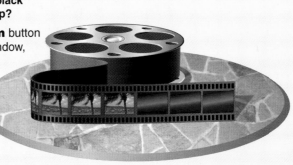) in the Project window,
and then click **Black
Video** in the
Object Type
list. Click **OK,**
and Premiere
places a new clip
of plain black footage
in the Project window.

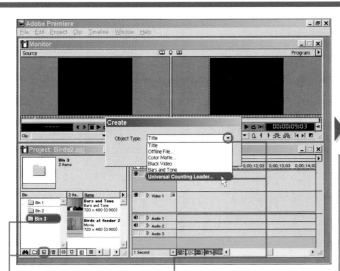

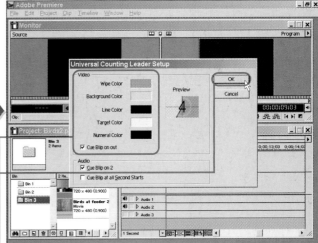

ADD A COUNTDOWN CLIP

1 Click the bin in which you
want to store a leader clip.

*Note: See Chapter 4 to organize
clips.*

2 Click the **Create Item**
button (▣).

■ The Create dialog box
appears.

3 Click ▾ to display object
types.

4 Click **Universal
Counting Leader**.

5 Click **OK**.

■ The Universal Counting
Leader Setup dialog box
appears.

6 Make any changes to the
settings, as needed.

7 Click **OK**.

■ Premiere adds a
Universal Counting Leader
clip to the Project window.

■ You can add the clip to
your project at any time.

*Note: See Chapter 8 to add a clip to
the Timeline.*

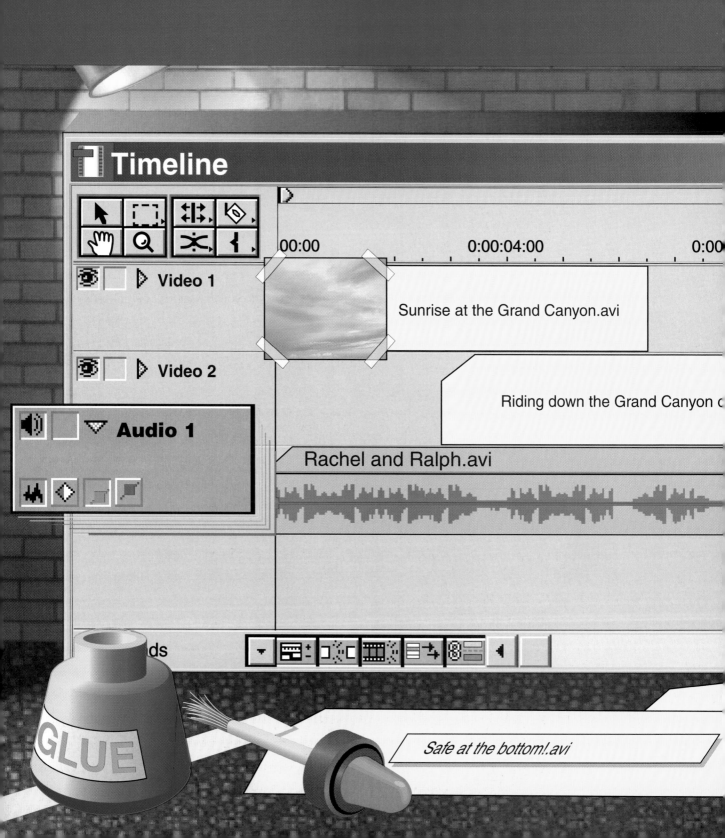

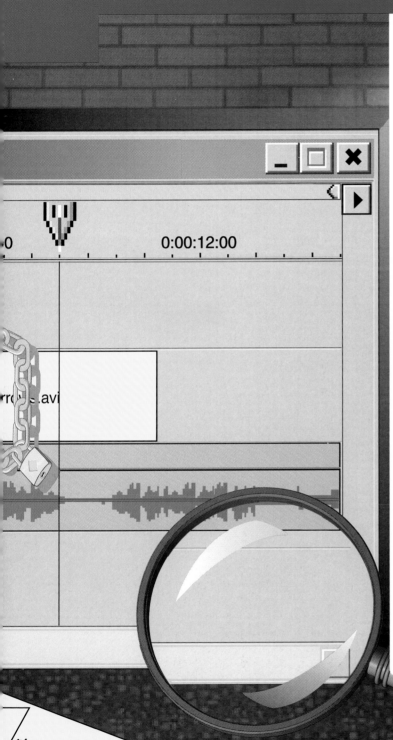

CHAPTER 6

Working with the Timeline

To start assembling your clips to create a video, you must understand a few things about the Premiere Timeline. This chapter shows you all the basics for using the Timeline window.

UNDERSTANDING THE TIMELINE

You can use the Timeline window to edit and assemble clips in your video project. To better understand how the Timeline works, first take a look at some of its features.

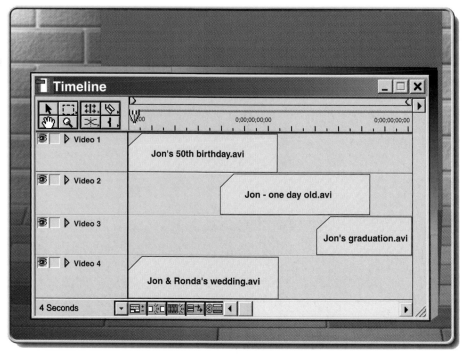

What Is the Timeline?

The Timeline window is a graphic, chronological representation of your video project. You can use the Timeline to arrange clips in the order you want them to appear.

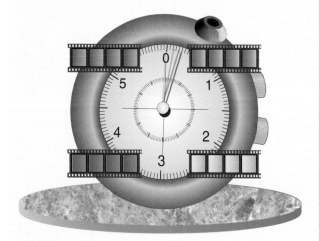

The Time Ruler

The top of the Timeline window shows a time ruler. Use the ruler to view in and out points of a clip as well as the length of the project. The Edit Line that appears on the time ruler marks the current edit point in the project.

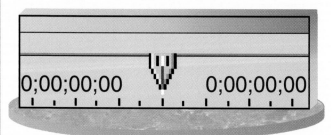

Tracks

Premiere uses tracks on the Timeline to hold your clips. You can have up to 99 video and 99 audio tracks, and you can add and remove tracks as needed. However, the tracks Video 1, Video 2, Transition, Audio 1, Audio 2, and Audio 3 cannot be deleted. These particular tracks are a permanent part of the Timeline window regardless of whether you use them.

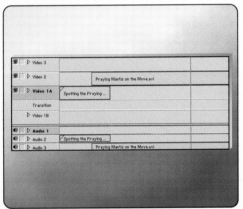

Types of Tracks

Use video tracks to hold clips, such as video, graphics, and title clips. You can add clips to a single track, or use multiple tracks. Audio tracks hold audio clips for your project. The Transition track, which appears in A/B editing mode, holds transitions you assign to segue from one clip to another.

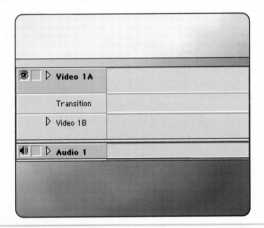

Hiding and Excluding Tracks

You can expand and collapse tracks in the Timeline window. You can also create *shy* tracks and exclude tracks. A shy track is hidden from view, but still remains a part of the project. You might create a shy track for a clip you have finished editing so you can "hide" it and concentrate on other clips. *Excluded* tracks are removed from the Timeline and are not previewed or exported with the video, but remain a part of the project.

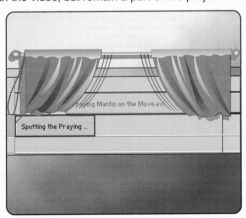

Workspace Settings

The Single-Track editing layout displays single-track video tracks in the Timeline. This layout is useful for cuts without transitions. The A/B editing layout turns Video Track 1 in the Timeline into two tracks, Video 1A and 1B, along with a Transition track between them. This layout is useful for creating transitions between clips.

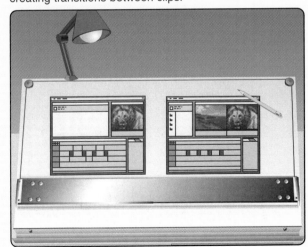

The Timeline is the backbone of your video project. Use the Timeline window to build your video, clip by clip. Take a moment and acquaint yourself with the parts of the Timeline window.

Toolbox

Contains tools for working with clips in the Timeline.

Work Area Markers

The markers can be dragged left or right to define the area on-screen that is previewed or exported.

Edit Line Marker

Marks the current edit point in the Timeline.

Video Track

Use tracks to hold clips you want to use to build your project.

Transition Track

Visible in A/B editing, use the Transition track to add transitions between clips.

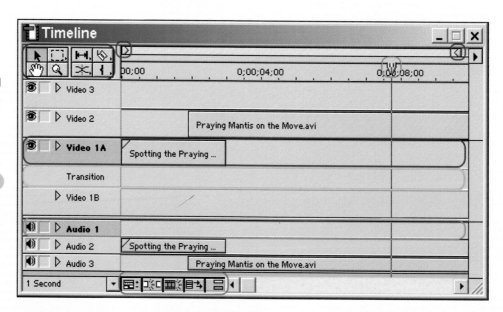

Audio Track

Use these tracks to hold audio clips.

Timeline Controls

Use these icon buttons to control how tracks are displayed.

Time Units

Use the Time Unit menu to change the way in which frames or seconds appear on the Timeline. By default, Premiere displays the Timeline in one-second intervals. You can view the Timeline in more or fewer intervals, or change the intervals to frames.

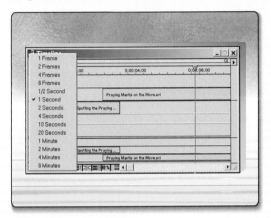

Timeline Menu

You can access commands related to the Timeline window using this handy menu. Check marks indicate the feature is turned on; no check mark means the feature is turned off.

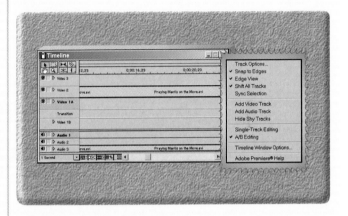

Moving Around the Timeline

Premiere lets you to move around the Timeline in many ways. You can use the Selector tool from the toolbox to drag clips around the Timeline. You can also use the Timeline's scroll bars to move your view. You can move the Edit Line marker to the frame you want to edit.

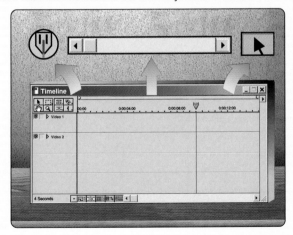

Using the Navigator Palette

Another way to navigate the Timeline is to use the Navigator palette. This palette gives you a bird's-eye view of the total Timeline for your project, and when you click an area in the palette, the Timeline immediately scrolls to that area.

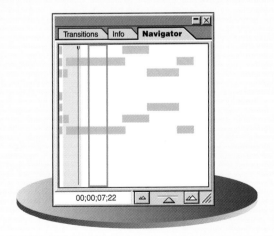

CUSTOMIZE THE TIMELINE

You can change how items appear in the Timeline window. For example, you may want to see a thumbnail image of the video clip as well as the clip name, or you may prefer a larger icon size.

CUSTOMIZE THE TIMELINE

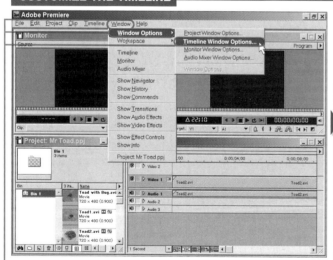

1 Click **Window**.

2 Click **Window Options**.

3 Click **Timeline Window Options**.

■ The Timeline Window Options dialog box opens.

*Note: You can also access the dialog box by clicking the **Timeline Window** menu and clicking **Timeline Window Options**.*

4 Click an icon size (○ changes to ⊙).

Note: A larger icon size makes it easier to see clips in the Timeline window.

5 Click a track format (○ changes to ⊙).

Other than using the Timeline
Window Options dialog box,
how else can I zoom my view
of the Timeline?

You can click the **Zoom Tool**
(🔍) in the Timeline window's
toolbox and click the Timeline
to quickly change the time unit
increments displayed.

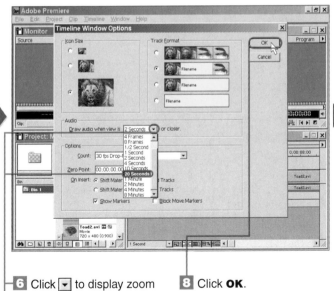

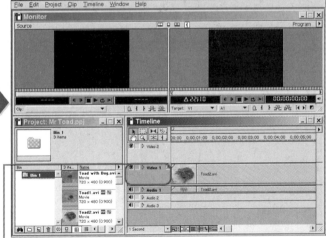

6 Click ⯆ to display zoom
level options.

7 Click a zoom level in
which to view audio
waveforms.

8 Click **OK**.

■ The Timeline changes to
reflect your choices.

ADD TRACKS

You can add tracks to the Timeline as you need them. By default, Premiere starts you off with two video tracks and three audio tracks. You may use as many as 99 of each in your project.

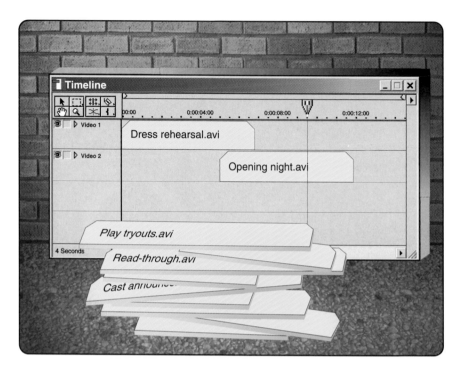

ADD TRACKS

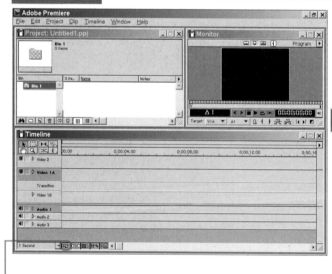

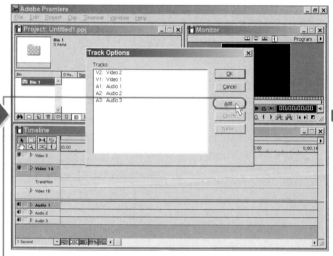

1 Click the **Track Options** button ().

■ The Track Options dialog box opens.

2 Click **Add**.

■ The Add Tracks dialog box opens.

Does Premiere provide a way to add a single video or audio track more quickly than using the Add Tracks dialog box?

You can click the **Timeline** menu and then click either **Add Video Track** or **Add Audio Track** to quickly insert a track. You can also click the Timeline window menu and click **Add Video Track** or **Add Audio Track**. You can even right-click over a track and click the commands from the pop-up menu.

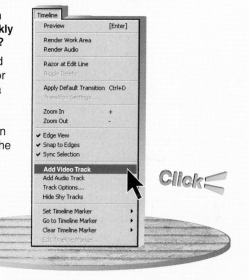

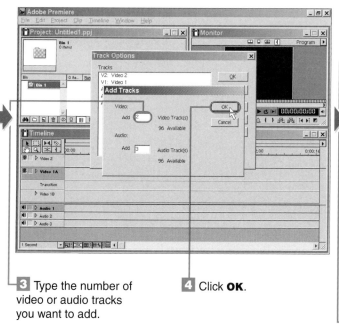

3 Type the number of video or audio tracks you want to add.

4 Click **OK**.

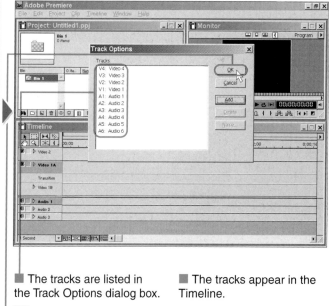

■ The tracks are listed in the Track Options dialog box.

5 Click **OK** again to exit the Track Options dialog box.

■ The tracks appear in the Timeline.

DELETE TRACKS

You can delete tracks that you no longer need. If the tracks use default names, Premiere renumbers the remaining tracks for you. You cannot delete the tracks Video 1 and 2, or Audio 1, 2, and 3.

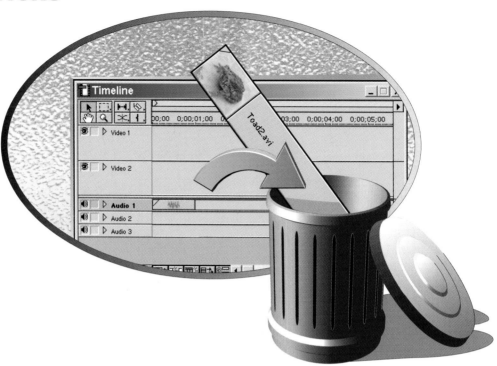

DELETE TRACKS

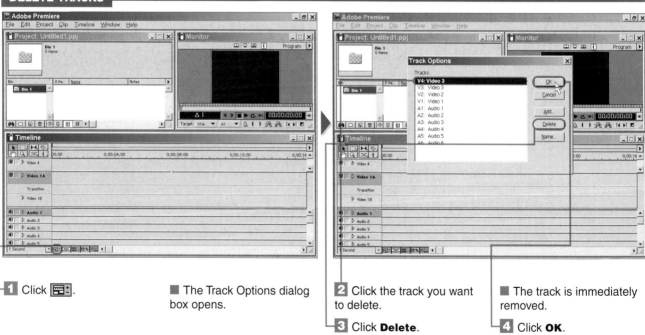

1 Click 📷.

■ The Track Options dialog box opens.

2 Click the track you want to delete.

3 Click **Delete**.

■ The track is immediately removed.

4 Click **OK**.

You can rename the
tracks displayed on the
Timeline to help you
better discern the
contents of each track.

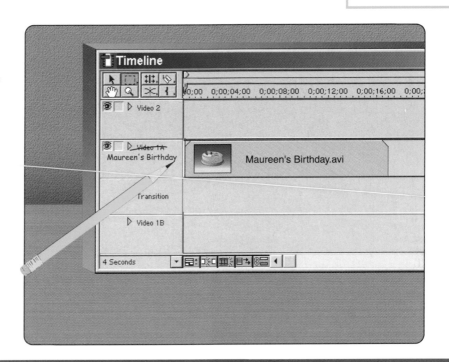

NAME TRACKS

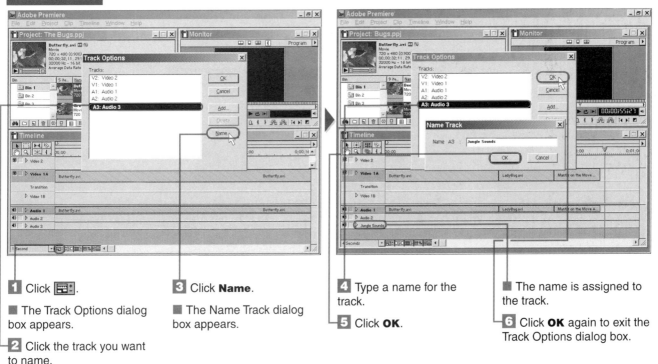

1 Click .

■ The Track Options dialog
box appears.

2 Click the track you want
to name.

3 Click **Name**.

■ The Name Track dialog
box appears.

4 Type a name for the
track.

5 Click **OK**.

■ The name is assigned to
the track.

6 Click **OK** again to exit the
Track Options dialog box.

LOCK AND UNLOCK TRACKS

You can protect the clips in a track by locking the track. This prevents you from making changes to the track. You cannot edit or move a locked track. To edit the track later, you can unlock it again.

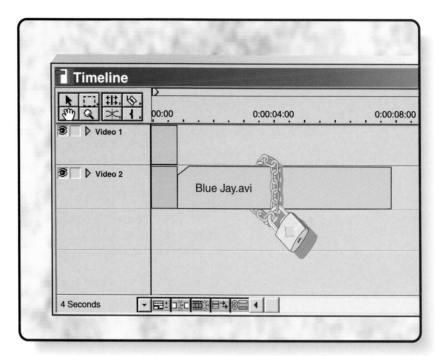

LOCK AND UNLOCK TRACKS

1 Click the **Lock** box (☐).

■ A 🔒 appears in the box, showing that the track is locked.

2 Click 🔒.

■ The track is unlocked.

EXPAND AND COLLAPSE TRACKS

You can expand tracks to view more information or additional controls. You can collapse tracks to maximize the Timeline space again. For example, if you expand an audio track, you can see the audio clip's waveform as well as fade and pan controls.

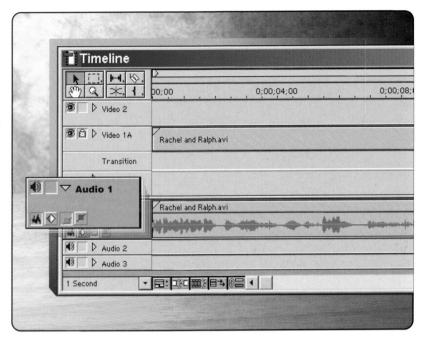

EXPAND AND COLLAPSE TRACKS

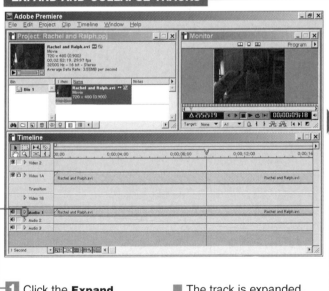

1 Click the **Expand** icon (▷).

■ The track is expanded.

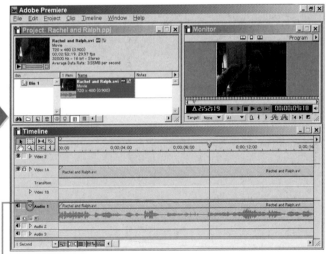

2 Click the **Collapse** icon (▽).

■ The track reverts to its collapsed state.

CREATE A SHY TRACK

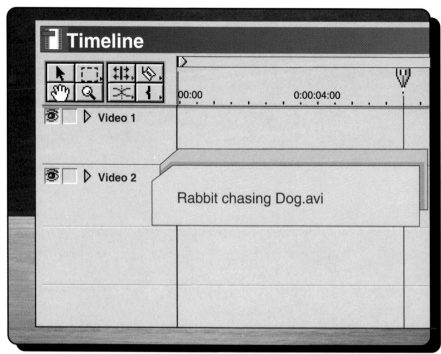

You can turn a track into a *shy track* to conserve Timeline space. Premiere hides shy tracks in the Timeline, but those tracks still remain part of the project. In the case of audio tracks, the audio is turned off. The content of shy tracks is still visible or audible, however, during playback.

CREATE A SHY TRACK

1 Press and hold **Ctrl** (Windows) or ⌘ (Mac).

2 Click 👁 for a video track or 🔊 for an audio track.

■ The 👁 or 🔊 turns white.

3 Click **Timeline**.

4 Click **Hide Shy Tracks**.

■ The shy tracks are hidden from view in the Timeline window.

*Note: To turn the tracks on again, click **Timeline**, **Show Shy Tracks**, and click the tracks again following steps **1** and **2**.*

EXCLUDE A TRACK

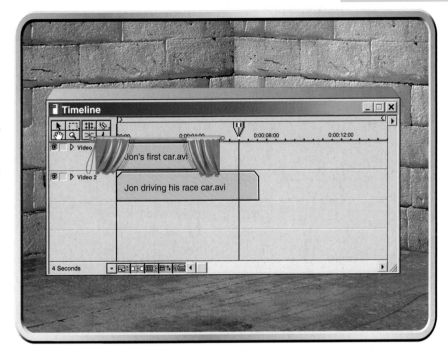

You can exclude a track to remove it from both the Timeline and from any playbacks and exports of the project. You may use the exclude track feature to create an export of the project without audio tracks, for example.

EXCLUDE A TRACK

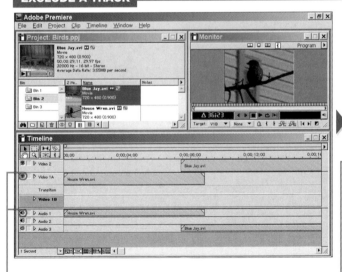

1 Click 🎬 for a video track or 🔊 for an audio track.

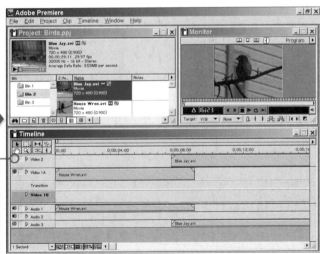

■ The box appears empty and the track is excluded.

Note: To turn the excluded track on again, repeat step 1.

USING THE NAVIGATOR PALETTE

The Navigator palette enables you to quickly move around the Timeline in longer video projects. The Navigator palette displays a bird's-eye view of the Timeline, and you can specify which area you want to view.

USING THE NAVIGATOR PALETTE

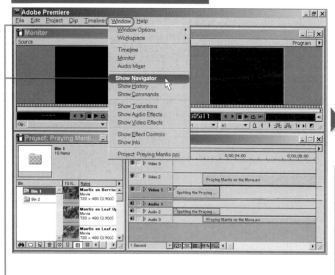

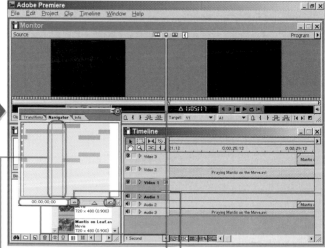

1 Click **Window**.

2 Click **Show Navigator**.

■ The Navigator palette opens.

3 Click and drag the view box to the Timeline area you want to view.

■ The Timeline immediately scrolls to the designated area.

■ Clicking these buttons changes the view box size.

■ To move a specific frame, type the timecode here.

■ To close the palette, click here.

You can zoom your view of the Timeline by changing the increments displayed on the Time Ruler. For example, a setting of 10 seconds causes more of the program to be displayed in the Timeline window than a setting of 0.5 seconds. You can view increments in frames or seconds on the Timeline.

ZOOM THE TIMELINE VIEW

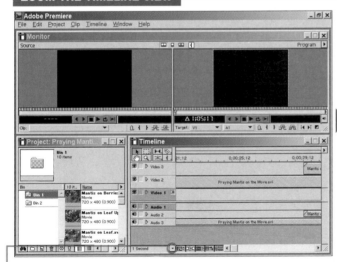

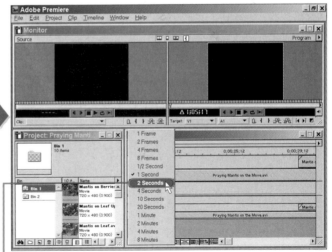

1 Click ⏷ to display a menu of time units.

2 Click the unit you want to assign to the Time Ruler.

■ The Timeline immediately reflects the new setting.

Note: You can also click 🔍 in the Toolbox and click over the Timeline to change increments.

CHAPTER 7

Editing in the Monitor Window

Do you want to learn how to edit clips in the Monitor window? This chapter shows you how.

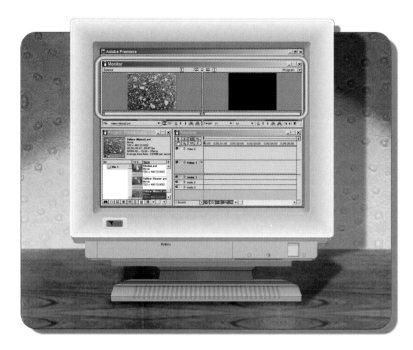

You can use the Monitor window to view your project as well as make edits to your clips. The Monitor window offers several different views. Based on the editing mode you use, the Monitor window shows a default view. If you use A/B editing, the window shows a single view. If you use Single-Track editing, the window shows dual view, both a Source view area and a Program view area.

Using Dual View

In dual view, you can view both the source clip and the program. Each side has playback controls. For many users, dual view is the view of choice when editing because it so closely resembles traditional videotape editing setups. Editors can see clips side by side, synchronize the clips, and check timing.

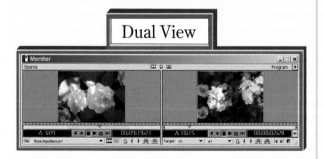

Using Single View

Single view, the default view for A/B editing, shows just the Program view. You can use this view to play back your video. Any source clips you view must be opened in a separate Clip window. Single view is useful when you do not need to see your source clips and want to focus only on the program. Single view also leaves screen space for you to open other features.

Using Trim Mode

Trim mode is useful when you want to make detailed adjustments in your video. Trim mode enables you to see two adjacent clips and make edits to the out and in points between the two. You can learn more about using Trim mode in Chapter 9.

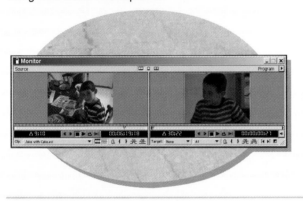

Using Playback Controls

The bottom of the Monitor window contains controls for playing the clip or program video. If you use Dual view, both the Source and Program areas have their own playback controls. Playback controls include buttons for moving back or forward one frame, stopping the clip or program, playing the clip or program, looping the clip, and playing a portion of the clip or program.

Edit Controls

Below the playback controls are controls for making edits to the clip or program. Among these controls are buttons for marking in and out points, moving between edits, lifting and extracting clips, and more.

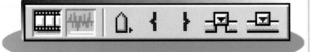

Program Details

The Monitor window gives you vital information about your project, such as listing the duration time of your video as well as the current location of the edit line in the program.

CHANGE MONITOR WINDOW VIEWS

You can change how you view the Monitor window in a project regardless of which editing mode you use. You can view the Monitor window in three ways: Dual view, Single view, or Trim Mode view. For example, if you use Single-Track edit mode, you may want to switch to Single view to focus on program playback.

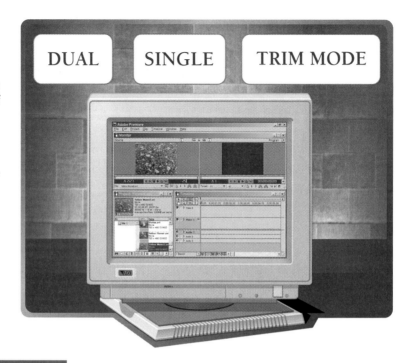

CHANGE MONITOR WINDOW VIEWS

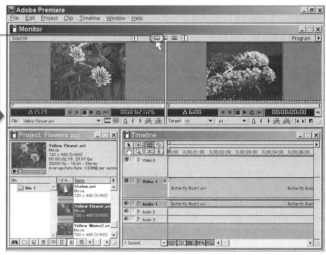

1 Open a project.

Note: See Chapter 2 to start a project.

2 Click a view mode button.

Note: See "Navigate the Monitor Window" to learn more about the different view modes.

■ Click **Dual View** (⊞) to see both a source and program area in the Monitor window.

How do I view my program in video safe zones?

Premiere displays the whole video frame in the Monitor window, but television monitors typically cut off the outer edges of the frame. To help you determine whether important parts of your video images appear within the TV crop area, you can tell Premiere to show video safe zones. Click the Monitor window menu and click a safe margin area. See the section "Using Video Safe Zones" to learn more.

■ You can click **Single View** (▢) to see only the program area in the Monitor window.

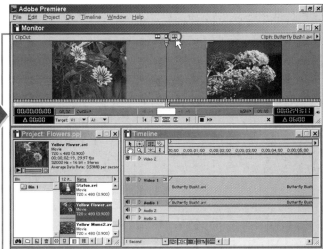

■ You can click **Trim Mode View** (▥) to see adjacent clips in the video.

VIEW A VIDEO CLIP IN SOURCE VIEW

In Single-Track edit mode, you can view and edit source clips in the Source view area of the Monitor window. After viewing and editing the clip, you can choose whether to add the clip to the project outline.

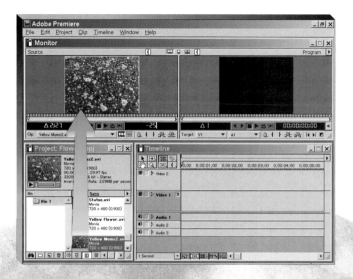

VIEW A VIDEO CLIP IN SOURCE VIEW

1 With a project open, click and drag the clip you want to view to the Source side of the Monitor window.

Note: See Chapters 3 and 4 to capture and import clips.

Note: See the next section, "View an Audio Clip in Source View," to view sound clips.

■ The clip appears in the Source area.

2 Click Play (▶) to play the clip.

■ Clicking here displays a list of recently viewed clips; you can click the one you want to revisit.

■ Clicking Loop (↻) plays the clip continuously.

■ Clicking Stop (■) stops the clip from playing.

In Single-Track edit mode, you can view and edit audio clips in the Source view area of the Monitor window. Audio clips appear as waveforms in the source view area. After viewing or editing the audio, you can choose whether to add the clip to the project outline.

VIEW AN AUDIO CLIP IN SOURCE VIEW

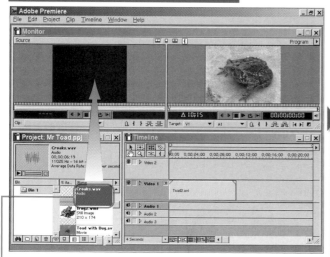

1 With a project open, click and drag the audio clip to the Source view side of the Monitor window.

Note: See Chapters 3 and 4 to capture and import clips.

Note: You must use Single-Track edit mode or Dual view to add clips to the Source view area of the Monitor window.

■ The clip appears in the Source view area.

2 Click ▶ to play the clip.

■ Clicking 🔁 plays the clip continuously.

■ Clicking ■ stops the clip from playing.

VIEW VIDEO IN PROGRAM VIEW

You can use the Program view area in Dual view or Single view to see the edited video play. For example, after assembling clips in the Timeline, you can preview the video project in the Program view area.

If you use Single-Track editing, the Monitor window is set to Dual view by default. If you use A/B editing, the Monitor window displays only the Program view area.

VIEW VIDEO IN PROGRAM VIEW

1 Open a project.

Note: See the section "Add a Source Clip to the Timeline" to assemble your project.

■ To play the video from a specific point in the project, click and drag the **Set Location** marker ( ) to the frame where you want to start playing.

2 Click ▶.

■ The video plays.

■ Clicking ■ stops the video from playing further.

You can change the
Monitor window's time
display for both the
Source and Program
views. By default, the
frame number of the
current source clip
appears in the time
readout display area.
You can change the
count to another time
display to suit your
editing needs.

SET THE TIME DISPLAY

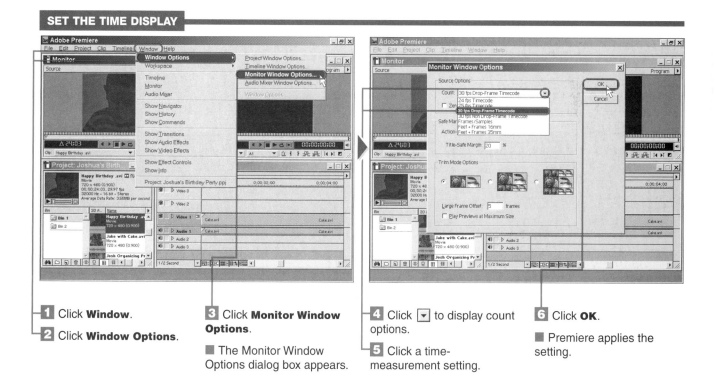

1 Click **Window**.

2 Click **Window Options**.

3 Click **Monitor Window
Options**.

■ The Monitor Window
Options dialog box appears.

4 Click ▼ to display count
options.

5 Click a time-
measurement setting.

6 Click **OK**.

■ Premiere applies the
setting.

USING VIDEO SAFE ZONES

You can change the Monitor window to display your video frames within *video safe zones*. Television monitors typically cut off the outer edges of video images. To ensure that all the important parts of your video are visible, switch to a video safe zone to see how the video plays.

USING VIDEO SAFE ZONES

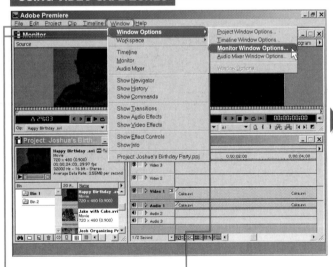

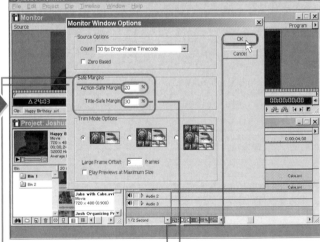

SET A SAFE MARGIN

1 Click **Window**.

2 Click **Window Options**.

3 Click **Monitor Window Options**.

■ The Monitor Window Options dialog box appears.

4 Set a safe zone margin.

■ You can type an action-safe value here.

■ You can type a title-safe value here.

Note: 90 percent of the image is considered to be action-safe; 80 percent is considered to be title-safe.

5 Click **OK**.

How do I know when to set video safe zones?

If you are worried your title text exceeds the viewable area for a television monitor, check the video using the video safe margins. The standard for title text is 80%, which means if the title text falls within 80% of the screen the text will be viewable. If the text extends beyond 80%, chances are the text will appear cut off.

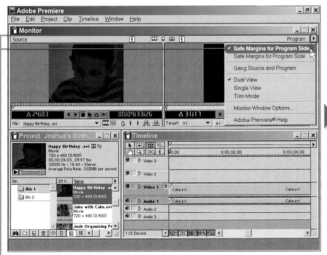

VIEW A SAFE ZONE

1 Click the Monitor window menu (▶).

2 Click a safe margin to view.

■ Clicking **Safe Margins for Source Side** shows the safe margins in the Source view.

■ Clicking **Safe Margins for Program Side** shows the safe margins in the Program view.

■ Premiere displays the safe margins.

■ This example shows safe margins in the Source view area.

CUE A CLIP IN THE MONITOR WINDOW

You can cue a clip in the Monitor window, either in Source view or Program view, using the Set Location marker. You can also cue a clip numerically by specifying an exact frame number, called *absolute time,* or you can add and subtract frames from the current point, called *relative time.*

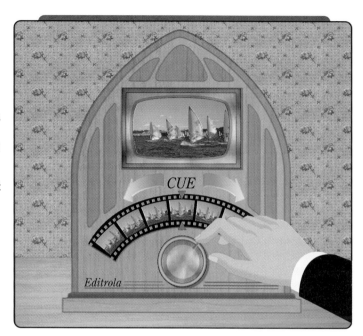

CUE A CLIP IN THE MONITOR WINDOW

CUE A CLIP WITH THE SET LOCATION MARKER

■1 With a project open, click and drag the **Set Location** marker ( ).

■ You can click and drag the Set Location marker in either Source view or Program view to cue the video.

■2 Stop dragging when you reach the frame you want to view.

■ The frame appears in the Source or Program view.

■ You can now play the video or perform an edit.

Note: See the sections "View a Video Clip in Source View" and "View Video in Program View" to play a clip.

Can I jump ahead or back a specified number of frames?

Yes. You can use the time display in either Source or Program view to cue the **Set Location** marker forward or backward. For example, if you type +25, Premiere moves the cue 25 frames forward. If you type –25, Premiere moves the cue 25 frames backward.

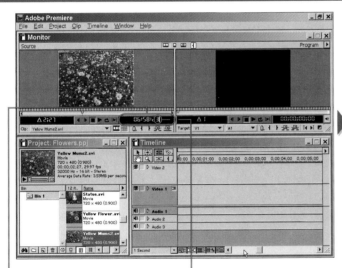

CUE A CLIP NUMERICALLY

1 Click the time display.

■ You can cue a source clip in Source view.

■ You can cue the video Program in Program view.

2 Type the frame number to which you want to cue the video.

■ You can use punctuation to type the frame number. For example, you can type **32:00**, **32;00**, or **32.00**.

■ The Set Location marker (🔽) moves to the designated frame in Source or Program view.

SET IN AND OUT POINTS IN THE MONITOR WINDOW

You can set in and out points in the Monitor window. Setting in and out points lets you trim the source clip to the length you want. The in point determines where the clip starts and the out point determines where the clip ends.

SET IN AND OUT POINTS IN THE MONITOR WINDOW

1 Add a clip to Source view.

Note: See the section "View a Video Clip in Source View" to learn more.

2 Click ▶ the clip to determine where you want to specify in and out points.

Note: You can set in and out points in the program view area to perform a three-point edit. See "Perform a Three-Point Edit" to learn more.

3 Click and drag the **Set Location** marker ( ) to the frame you want to set as the in point.

Note: See the section "Cue a Clip in the Monitor Window" to learn more.

4 Click the **Mark In** button ( ).

■ An in point icon ( ) appears at the current frame.

■ The time readout shows the frame number.

How do I set separate in and out points for the audio portion of the clip?

Audio that was captured along with the video footage is linked to the video clip. To perform a separate edit, you can unlink the two clips or you can perform a split edit. See Chapter 8 to learn how to unlink two clips. See Chapter 9 to learn how to perform a split edit.

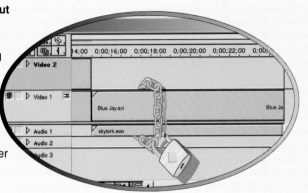

5 Click and drag the **Set Location** marker (🔲) to the frame you want to set as the out point.

6 Click the **Mark Out** button (🔲).

■ An out point icon (🔲) appears at the current frame.

■ The time readout shows the frame number.

7 Click the **Play In to Out** button (🔲) to play the clip in Source view.

■ You can click and drag an in or out point to adjust its location.

■ The clip's duration appears here.

■ You can now add the clip to the Timeline.

Note: See "Add a Source Clip to the Timeline" to add clips to the Timeline window.

ADD A SOURCE CLIP TO THE TIMELINE

After you edit a source
clip in the Monitor
window, you can add it
to the Timeline.

ADD A SOURCE CLIP TO THE TIMELINE

1 Edit a clip in Source view.

*Note: See "Set In and Out Points in
the Monitor Window" to edit a clip in
Source view.*

2 Click and drag the clip to
the desired unused track in
the Timeline (becomes
).

*Note: To add the video portion of the
clip only, click . To add only the
audio portion of the clip, click .*

■ The clip appears in the
Timeline.

*Note: See Chapter 6 to learn about
Timeline tracks.*

After you edit a source clip in the Monitor window, you can add it to a specific track in the Timeline window. By targeting a track, you tell Premiere exactly where you want the clip to be inserted.

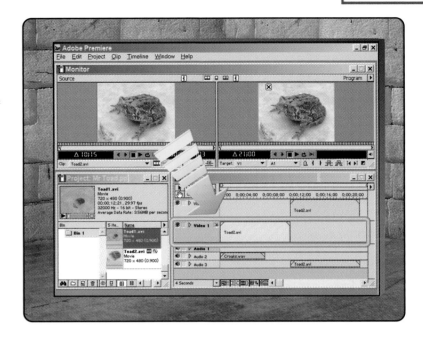

SPECIFY A TARGET TRACK

1 Click and drag the **Edit Line** (📷) to where you want the clip inserted.

Note: See Chapter 6 to learn about the Timeline.

2 Edit a clip in Source view.

Note: See "Set In and Out Points in the Monitor Window" to edit a clip in Source view.

3 Click ▾.

4 Click the track to which you want to add the clip.

■ The clip appears in the Timeline window.

Note: See Chapter 6 to learn about Timeline tracks.

ADD SOURCE MARKERS

You can use markers to identify points in the source clip. For example, you may add a source marker to identify where a title should fade. You can add numbered or unnumbered markers, and you can also add comment text to a marker.

Source markers are reference points and do not appear in the actual video.

ADD SOURCE MARKERS

SET A SOURCE MARKER

1 Cue a source clip to the frame where you want to add a marker.

Note: See the section "View a Video Clip in Source View" to view source clips.

2 Click the **Marker Menu** button (🔲).

3 Click **Mark**.

4 Click the type of marker you want to set.

■ The marker appears above the source clip.

■ You can identify key parts of a clip with numbered and unnumbered markers. For example, you may use numbered markers to mark several possible edit points.

124

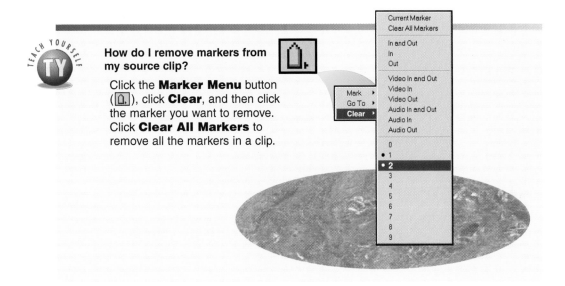

How do I remove markers from my source clip?

Click the **Marker Menu** button (📭), click **Clear**, and then click the marker you want to remove. Click **Clear All Markers** to remove all the markers in a clip.

CUE A SOURCE MARKER

1 Load a source clip containing the marker in Source view.

2 Click the **Marker Menu** button (📭).

3 Click **Go To**.

4 Click the marker you want to cue in Source view.

■ The Source view Set Location marker (🎬) immediately scrolls to the designated frame.

PERFORM A THREE-POINT EDIT

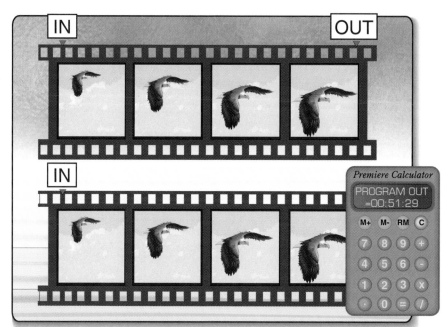

You can create a *three-point edit* in the Monitor window that replaces a range of frames in the program view area with a specified range of frames you designate in source view. Perform a three-point edit when one of the clip's in or out points is critical but the other is not. Use Dual view to perform this type of edit.

PERFORM A THREE-POINT EDIT

1 Add a clip to Source view.

Note: See "View a Video Clip in Source View" to add source clips.

2 Choose a target track for the clip.

Note: See "Specify a Target Track" to set a target track.

3 Specify three in and out points — either two in and one out point, or two out and one in point — in both Source and Program view.

Note: See "Set In and Out Points in the Monitor Window" to add in and out points.

Do I have to specify an in or out point in program view?

No. You can cue the **Edit Line** 🔱 in the Timeline window to mark where you want the clip inserted as an end or out point. See Chapter 8 to learn how to cue the **Edit Line**.

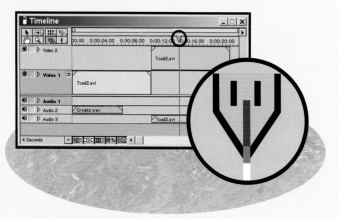

⬛4 Click an edit button.

⬛ Clicking **Insert** (🔳) inserts the clip and shifts other clips over to accommodate the new clip.

⬛ Clicking **Overlay** (🔳) overwrites any existing clips with the new clip.

Note: Make sure the existing clips in the Timeline track are not locked. See Chapter 6 to unlock a track. See Chapter 8 to unlock clips.

⬛ The edited clip appears in the Timeline.

PERFORM A FOUR-POINT EDIT

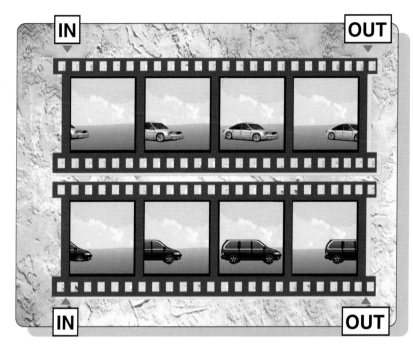

You can specify a *four-point edit* in the Monitor window that replaces a range of frames in the video program view area with a specified range of frames you designate in source view. Perform a four-point edit when you want to designate all four edit points.

PERFORM A FOUR-POINT EDIT

1 Add a clip to Source view.

Note: See "View a Video Clip in Source View" to add source clips.

2 Specify a target track for the clip.

Note: See "Specify a Target Track" to set a target track.

3 Specify the four edit points in both the Source and Program views.

Note: See "Set In and Out Points in the Monitor Window" to create in and out points.

How do I check a clip's speed?

You can see the speed of a clip using the Info palette. Click the clip you want to check in the Timeline window, click **Window**, and then click **Show Info**. The Info palette appears with details about the clip, including the clip speed and duration.

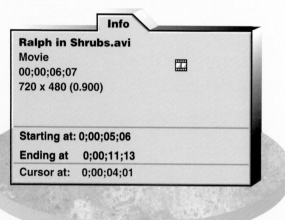

Info

Ralph in Shrubs.avi
Movie
00;00;06;07
720 x 480 (0.900)

Starting at: 0;00;05;06

Ending at   0;00;11;13

Cursor at: 0;00;04;01

4 Click an edit button.

■ Clicking **Insert** ( ) inserts the clip and shift other clips over to accommodate the new clip.

■ Clicking **Overlay** ( ) overwrites any existing clips with the new clip.

Note: Make sure the existing clips in the Timeline track are not locked. See Chapter 6 to unlock a track. See Chapter 8 to unlock clips.

■ If the source points and the program points differ, the Fit Clip dialog box appears.

■ Clicking **Change Speed** makes the source clip fit within the program's in and out points.

■ Clicking **Trim Source** changes the source out point to match the program out point.

■ The edited clip appears in the Timeline window.

LIFT AND EXTRACT FRAMES

You can remove segments of clips from a video using controls found in the Monitor window's program view area. Premiere lets you remove frames and leave a gap, or remove frames along with the gap.

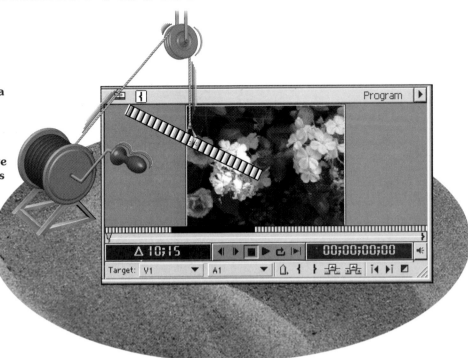

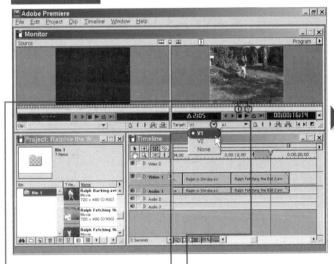

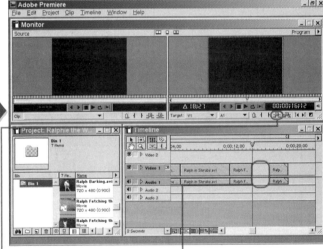

1 Set the in and out points for the portion of video you want to remove.

Note: See "Set In and Out Points in the Monitor Window" to set in and out points.

2 Click ▾ to display available target tracks.

3 Click the track from which you want to remove frames.

4 Click the **Lift** button (⊞).

■ The frames between the designated in and out points are cleared, leaving empty frames in their place.

I cannot lift or extract frames. Why not?

Make sure that the existing clips in the Timeline track are not locked. You cannot lift or extract frames from a locked track or clip. See Chapter 6 to learn how to unlock a track. See Chapter 8 to learn how to unlock clips.

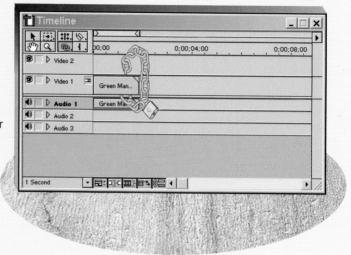

EXTRACT FRAMES

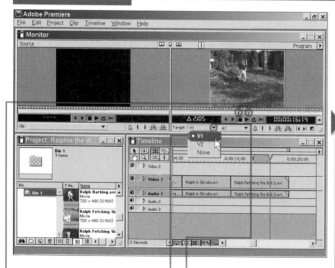

1 With a project open, set the in and out points for the portion of video you want to remove.

Note: See "View Video in Program View" to view the project.

2 Click ▾ to display available tracks.

3 Click the track from which you want to remove frames.

4 Click the **Extract** button (🔲).

■ The frames between the designated in and out points are cleared, including the frames themselves.

PREVIEW A VIDEO PROJECT

As you edit and assemble your video, you can preview it in the Monitor window's Program view area. To preview the video with edits and effects applied, Premiere must first build a copy of the video. Depending on the size of the file, this process may take a only few seconds or several minutes.

PREVIEW A VIDEO PROJECT

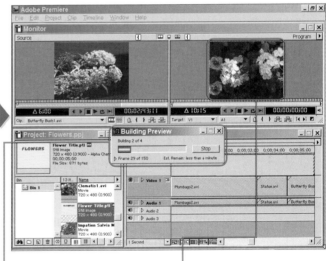

PREVIEW THE ENTIRE VIDEO

1 Cue the **Edit Line** marker (▓) to the beginning of the Timeline.

Note: See Chapter 6 to learn about the Timeline.

2 Click **Timeline**.

3 Click **Preview**.

■ You can also press **Enter** (Windows) or **Return** (Mac).

■ Premiere builds the preview file.

■ The video program plays.

Can I create a preview file without viewing it right away?

Yes. Preparing a preview file can save you time so it is ready to play when you want to view the project. Click **Timeline** and then **Render Work Area**. Premiere builds the preview file, which you can view at any time by pressing **Enter** (Windows) or **Return** (Mac).

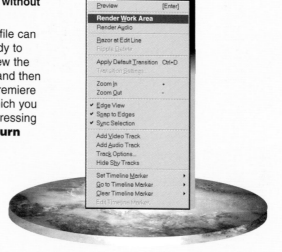

PREVIEW A PORTION OF THE VIDEO

■1 Drag ▷ and ◁ over the area you want to preview.

■ You can click and drag the work area markers to specify where the work area begins or ends.

Note: See Chapter 6 to learn more about working with the Timeline window.

■2 Click **Timeline**.

■3 Click **Preview**.

■ You can also press **Enter** (Windows) or **Return** (Mac).

■ Premiere builds the preview file.

■ The video program plays.

GANG THE SOURCE AND PROGRAM VIEWS

You can preview the relationship between the source clip and program view. Called *ganging*, this process synchronizes the clips so that you can see how both are playing and where you may need to further adjust the edits.

GANG THE SOURCE AND PROGRAM VIEWS

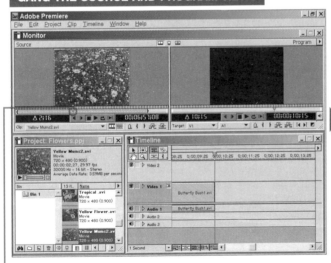

1 Cue the source clip to the frame you want to synchronize.

Note: See the section "Cue a Clip in the Monitor Window" to cue clips.

2 Cue the Program view to the frame you want to synchronize.

What exactly is ganging?

Ganging is simply viewing both the source clip and the program at the same time. The term comes from traditional editing, where an editor gangs monitors to see a clip play in one monitor while the program played in the other. The editor could then decide whether to actually add the clip to the master video.

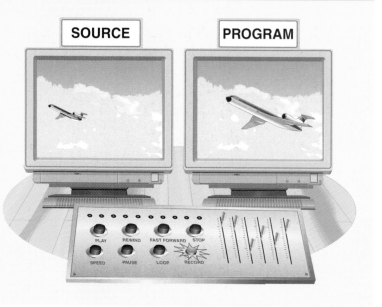

SOURCE

PROGRAM

PLAY   REWIND   FAST FORWARD   STOP

SPEED   PAUSE   LOOP   RECORD

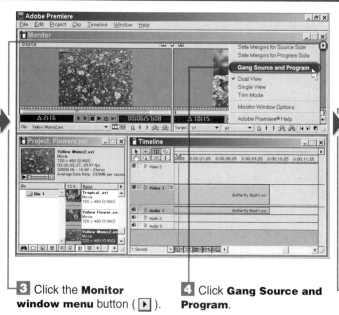

3 Click the **Monitor window menu** button (▶).

4 Click **Gang Source and Program**.

5 Click and drag the **Set Location** marker (🔽) back and forth in either view to see the frames move in synch.

■ Clicking ▶ turns off the gang feature.

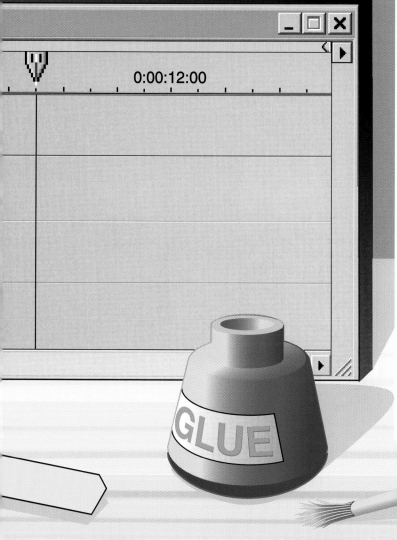

CHAPTER 8

Editing Clips in the Timeline

Are you ready to start assembling your video? This chapter guides you through techniques for adding and editing clips on the Timeline.

0:00:12:00

GLUE

USING THE TIMELINE TOOLBOX TOOLS

While editing your video, you can use the editing tools found in the Timeline window's toolbox. The toolbox includes two sets of buttons, one set for selecting and viewing clips in the Timeline and another set for editing clips. Not all tools are visible all the time. Several of the buttons share space with other buttons. By default, only one button appears in the shared group, but you can expand the group to see all the buttons and activate another button.

USING THE TIMELINE TOOLBOX TOOLS

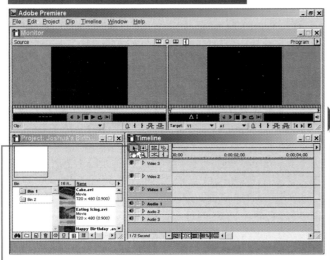

1 With a project open, click the tool you want to use.

■ Depending on the tool, takes another shape.

2 If the tool button shows a tiny arrow icon, click and hold over the button to view all of the buttons.

3 Click the tool you want to use.

■ You can now use the selected tool to make an edit.

Note: To avoid unnecessary edits, always click the Selection tool ( ) after using the other tools.

138

CUE THE EDIT LINE

You can cue the
Edit Line to a
particular frame
in the Timeline.
You can also cue
the Edit Line to
start playing the
program preview
from a specific
point in the video.

CUE THE EDIT LINE

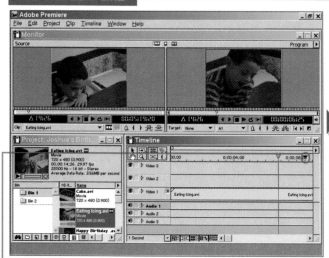

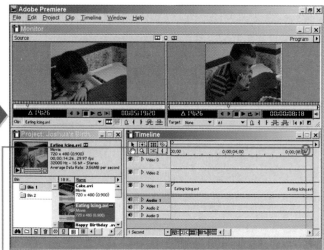

1 With a project open, click
the Timeline ruler where you
want to move the Edit Line
(⬚ becomes ▼).

■ You can also click and
drag the Edit Line (▼) to a
new point.

■ Premiere immediately
moves the Edit Line.

*Note: To play the video from the
timeline, click and drag ▼ back and
forth on the Timeline ruler. The video
plays in the Monitor window.*

■ The Monitor window
changes to show the new
frame location.

ADD A CLIP TO THE TIMELINE

You can add clips to the Timeline window to assemble your video. Whether you capture clips or use existing clips, you can place clips into tracks on the Timeline to sequentially build a video project. Add video, still image, and title clips to video tracks in the Timeline. You can also add sound clips to audio tracks.

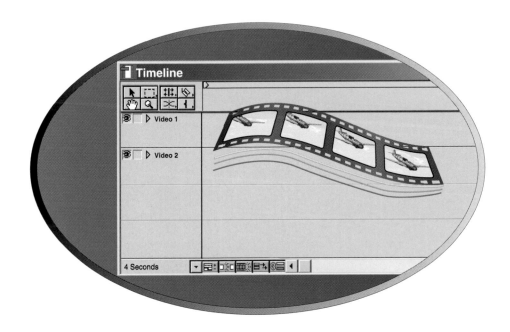

ADD A CLIP TO THE TIMELINE

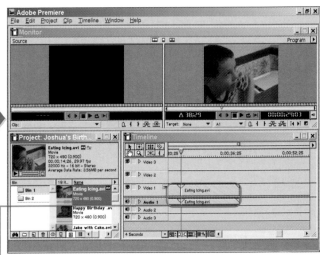

1 Locate the clip you want to add.

Note: See Chapters 3 and 4 to capture and import clips.

2 Click and drag the clip to the track in which you want it inserted (▷ becomes ✍️).

Note: See Chapter 7 to trim and add source clips using the Monitor window.

■ The clip appears in the Timeline.

Note: See Chapter 7 to preview a video.

You can select a clip in the Timeline window in order to perform edits on the clip.

You must select a clip to move it on the Timeline or delete it.

SELECT A CLIP IN THE TIMELINE

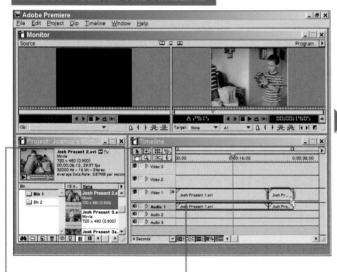

■ 1 Click the clip you want to select.

■ If you were previously using another tool from the Timeline toolbox, click ▲.

■ To select multiple clips, press and hold **Ctrl** while clicking clips.

Note: See the previous section, "Add a Clip to the Timeline," to place clips on the Timeline.

■ The clip is highlighted with dashed lines in the Timeline.

■ If the clip includes audio, Premiere selects the linked audio clip as well.

Note: See the section "Link and Unlink Clips" to learn more about linked clips.

■ 2 Click elsewhere in the Timeline to deselect the clip.

DELETE A CLIP FROM THE TIMELINE

You can delete a clip from the Timeline that you no longer need. Deleting a clip from the Timeline window does not remove the clip from the project file. The clip remains listed in the Project window.

DELETE A CLIP FROM THE TIMELINE

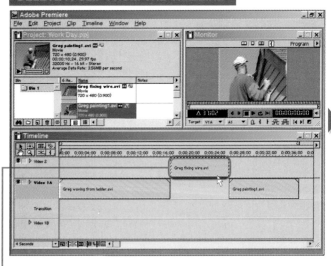

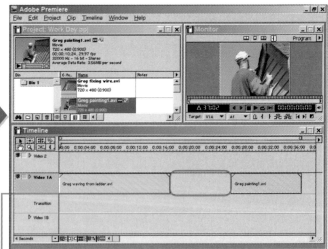

1 Click the clip you want to remove.

Note: See the section "Add a Clip to the Timeline" to place clips on the Timeline.

2 Press Delete.

■ The clip is removed from the Timeline.

Note: See the section "Delete a Gap Between Clips" to remove gaps in the Timeline.

REUSE A CLIP

You can reuse the same clip in multiple places throughout the Timeline. The original clip is called the *master clip* and all duplicates are *instances* of that master clip. If you delete a master clip, Premiere deletes all duplicates.

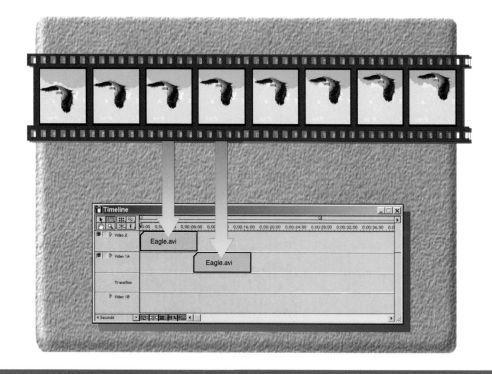

REUSE A CLIP

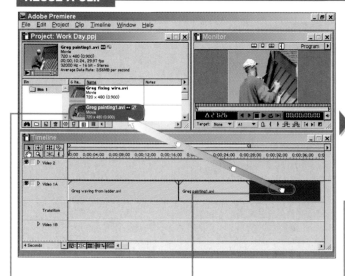

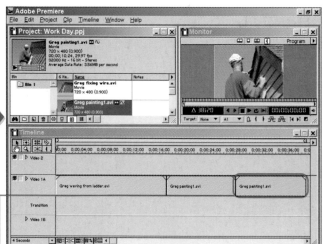

1 Click the clip you want to reuse.

Note: See Chapter 2 to work with the Project window.

2 Click and drag the clip to another location on the Timeline (becomes 🖑).

Note: See the section "Add a Clip to the Timeline" to place clips on the Timeline.

■ A duplicate of the clip appears in the Timeline.

*Note: To create two copies of the same clip in the Project window, click the clip, click **Edit**, and then click **Duplicate Clip**.*

MOVE CLIPS IN THE TIMELINE

You can move a clip in the Timeline to another spot on the same track or to another track entirely. You can also move multiple clips or every clip at once.

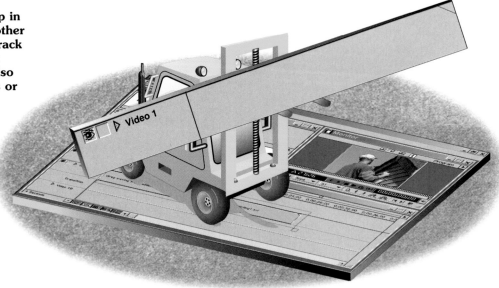

MOVE CLIPS IN THE TIMELINE

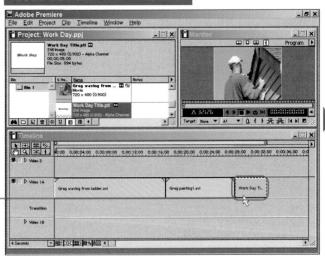

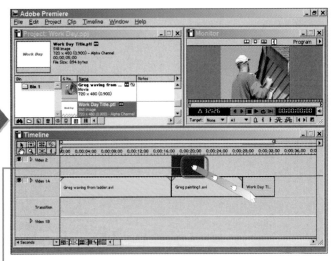

MOVE A SINGLE CLIP

1 Click the clip you want to move.

Note: See the section "Select a Clip in the Timeline" to select clips.

Note: See the section "Add a Clip to the Timeline" to place clips on the Timeline.

2 Click and drag the clip to a new location (⟋ becomes ✎).

■ The clip is moved.

Note: See Chapter 6 to work with Timeline tracks.

Can I move just a few tracks?

Yes. You can move a range of tracks using the **Range Select** tool. Click 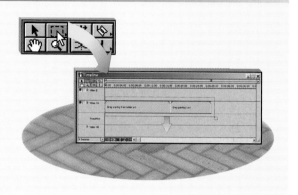 in the toolbox and then click and drag a box around the clips you want to move. Finally, drag the range to an unused area on the Timeline and drop it in place.

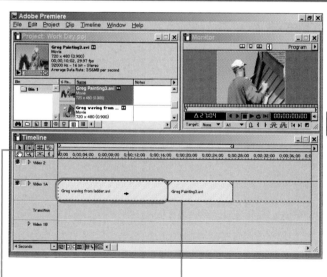

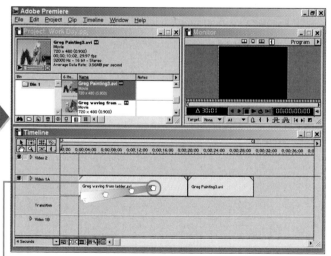

MOVE ALL THE CLIPS IN A TRACK

1 Click the **Track Select** tool (▦).

Note: See the section "Using the Timeline Toolbox Tools" to activate tool buttons.

2 Click the first clip in the track of clips you want to move (◽ becomes ➜).

■ All the clips in the track are selected.

3 Click and drag the clips to a new location (◽ becomes ✋).

■ The clips are moved.

Note: See Chapter 6 to work with Timeline tracks.

145

DELETE A GAP BETWEEN CLIPS

You can remove any gaps that appear between clips in a track. Often in the course of assembling and moving clips, gaps occur. You can quickly remove a gap using a *Ripple Delete* edit.

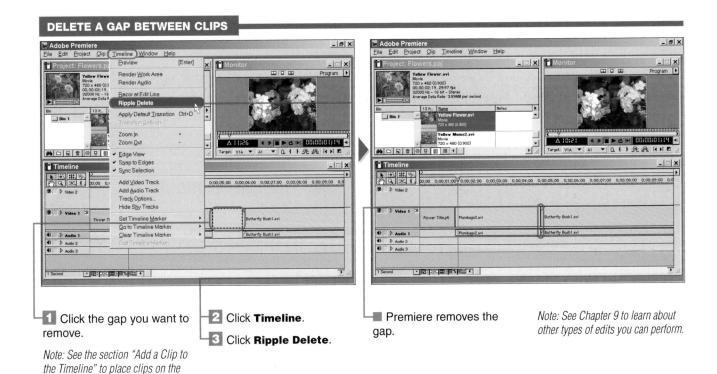

DELETE A GAP BETWEEN CLIPS

1 Click the gap you want to remove.

Note: See the section "Add a Clip to the Timeline" to place clips on the Timeline.

2 Click **Timeline**.

3 Click **Ripple Delete**.

■ Premiere removes the gap.

Note: See Chapter 9 to learn about other types of edits you can perform.

You can lock a clip in place on the Timeline and then unlock it when you need to edit or move it. Locking a clip prevents you from making accidental changes to the clip. Locked clips appear with a pattern of diagonal slashes on the Timeline.

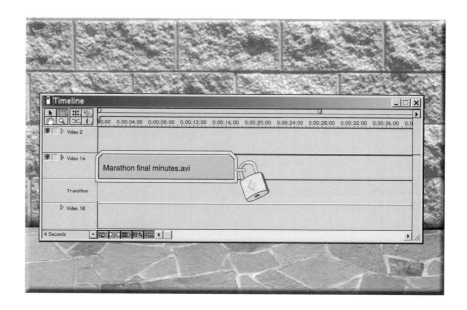

LOCK AND UNLOCK CLIPS

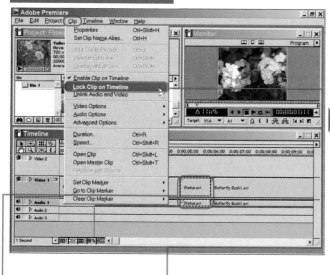

1 Click the clip you want to lock.

Note: See the section "Add a Clip to the Timeline" to place clips on the Timeline.

2 Click **Clip**.

3 Click **Lock Clip on Timeline**.

■ The clip is locked.

■ Locked clips appear with slash marks on the Timeline.

■ To unlock a locked clip, repeat steps **1** through **3**.

Note: See Chapter 6 to work with Timeline tracks.

DISABLE OR ENABLE A CLIP

You can disable a clip to prevent it from playing in the video preview or from exporting when you output your project. You may disable a clip when you want to temporarily keep it from playing. For example, you might disable an audio clip so you can concentrate on the video images. You can enable a clip to include it again later.

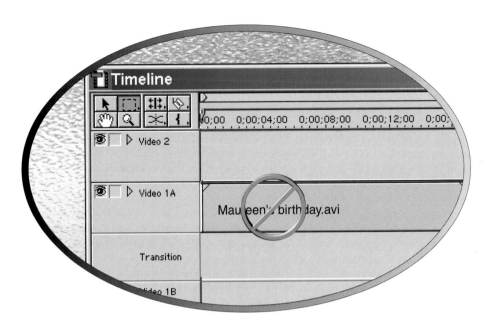

DISABLE OR ENABLE A CLIP

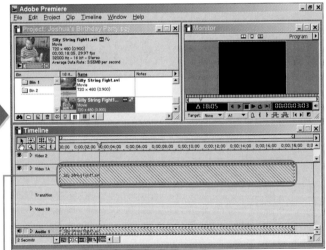

1 Click the clip you want to disable.

Note: See the section "Add a Clip to the Timeline" to place clips on the Timeline.

2 Click **Clip**.

3 Click **Enable Clip on Timeline**.

■ A check mark next to the command name indicates the clip is enabled. No check mark means the clip is disabled.

■ The clip is disabled.

■ Disabled clips appear with backward slash marks on the Timeline.

■ To enable a disabled clip, repeat steps **1** through **3**.

Note: See Chapter 6 to work with Timeline tracks.

USING SNAP TO EDGES

You can use the Snap to Edges feature to help you move and align clips in the Timeline tracks. When the feature is activated, clips snap to the edges of other clips much like a magnet when you move them. If you turn the feature off, you can move clips independently. You can toggle the feature on or off as needed.

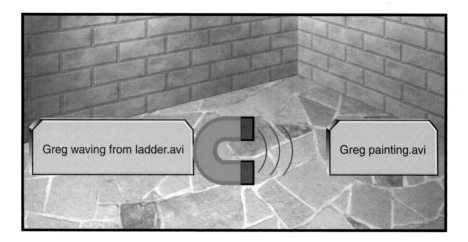

USING SNAP TO EDGES

1 Click the **Snap to Edges** toggle button (changes to).

Note: See Chapter 6 to work with Timeline tracks.

2 Click and drag a clip toward the edge of another clip (becomes).

■ The clip snaps to the edges of the other clip.

Note: See the section "Move Clips in the Timeline" to move clips around in the Timeline.

LINK AND UNLINK CLIPS

You can link and unlink clips in the Timeline to let you work with them separately or at the same time. For example, some clips include both video and audio, which appear in separate tracks but are linked. You may need to unlink the audio clip, for example, to move it to another part of the project. You can only link video to audio, not to other video clips.

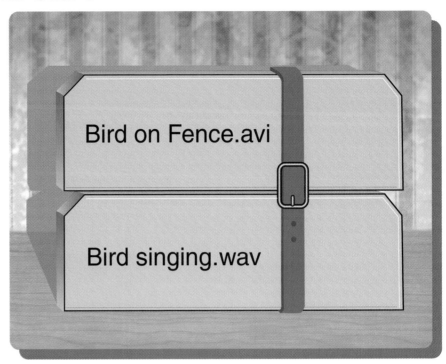

LINK CLIPS

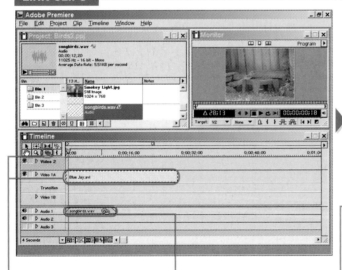

1 With a project open, click the **Link/Unlink** tool ( ).

2 Click the first clip you want to link.

Note: See the section "Add a Clip to the Timeline" to place clips on the Timeline.

3 Click the second clip you want to link to (becomes).

■ Premiere links the clips, which you can now move at the same time.

Note: See the section "Move Clips in the Timeline" to move clips around the Timeline tracks.

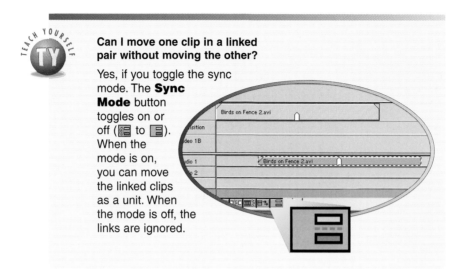

Can I move one clip in a linked pair without moving the other?

Yes, if you toggle the sync mode. The **Sync Mode** button toggles on or off (🔳 to 🔲). When the mode is on, you can move the linked clips as a unit. When the mode is off, the links are ignored.

UNLINK CLIPS

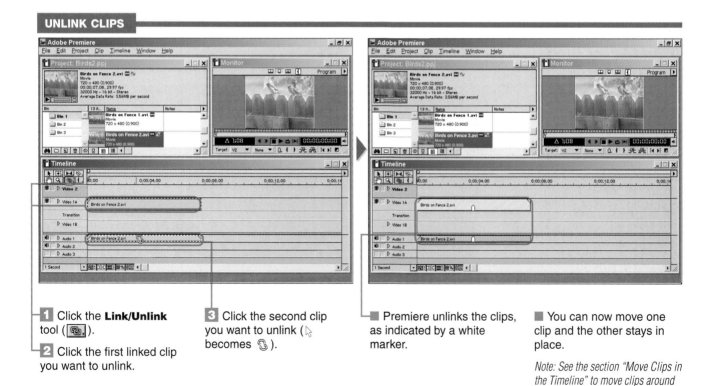

1 Click the **Link/Unlink** tool (🔗).

2 Click the first linked clip you want to unlink.

3 Click the second clip you want to unlink (↖ becomes ☍).

■ Premiere unlinks the clips, as indicated by a white marker.

■ You can now move one clip and the other stays in place.

Note: See the section "Move Clips in the Timeline" to move clips around the Timeline tracks.

CUT AND PASTE CLIPS

You can cut and paste clips to move them around the Timeline. Using the Paste to Fit command, you can make a clip fit a predetermined spot in the Timeline.

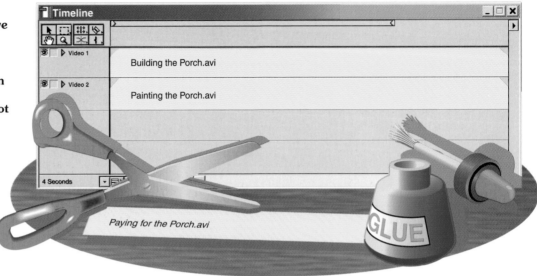

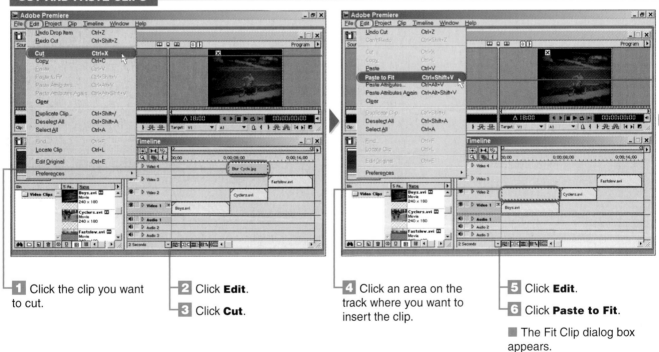

1 Click the clip you want to cut.

2 Click **Edit**.

3 Click **Cut**.

4 Click an area on the track where you want to insert the clip.

5 Click **Edit**.

6 Click **Paste to Fit**.

■ The Fit Clip dialog box appears.

Can I copy and paste clips?

Yes. Copying a clip duplicates it on the Timeline. After you select the clip you want to copy, click **Edit** and then **Copy**. Click the track where you want to insert the clip, and then click **Edit**, followed by **Paste**. A copy appears. If you click **Paste to Fit** in the **Edit** menu, the Fit Clip dialog box, shown in step **7** below, appears and you can specify how you want the copy pasted.

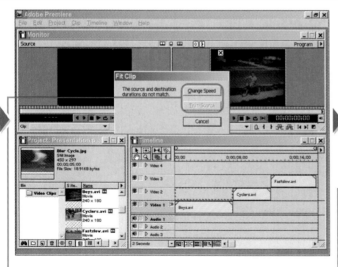

7 Click an option.

■ Clicking **Change Speed** makes the clip fit by changing the speed of the clip.

■ Clicking **Trim Source** trims the source out point to make the clip fit.

─ ■ Premiere pastes the clip in place.

Note: See Chapter 7 to preview a video.

SPLIT CLIPS

You can cut a clip into two or more pieces to apply an effect to one part and not the other. For example, you may want to split a clip into two to move a segment to another track in the Timeline.

SPLIT A SINGLE CLIP

1 Display the clip you want to cut in the Timeline.

2 Click the **Razor** tool (⬚) (⬚ becomes ◈).

Note: See the section "Using the Timeline Toolbox Tools" to activate tool buttons.

3 Click the clip where you want the split to occur.

■ The clip immediately splits into two.

Note: See the section "Move Clips in the Timeline" to move clips.

I mistakenly split a clip in the wrong spot. How do I undo the split?

Click **Edit**, then **Undo** immediately after performing the split. Premiere keeps track of your edits and lists them in the History palette. To display the palette, click **Window**, **Show**, and then **History**. Click an edit in the list and all edits performed after the selected edit, including the selected edit, are undone.

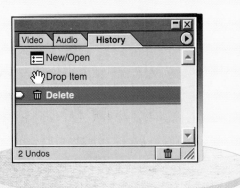

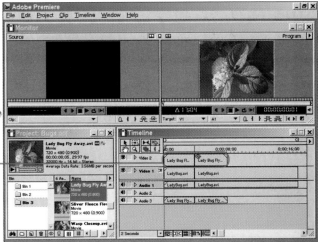

SPLIT MULTIPLE CLIPS

1 Locate the clips you want to cut.

2 Click the **Multiple Razor** tool ( ) (becomes).

Note: See the section "Using the Timeline Toolbox Tools" to activate tool buttons.

3 Click where in the Timeline you want the splits to occur.

■ The clips are immediately split.

Note: See the section "Move Clips in the Timeline" to move clips.

SET IN AND OUT POINTS ON THE TIMELINE

You can set in and out points for a clip in the Timeline window. Setting in and out points enables you to trim a clip to the exact length you want. The in point determines where the clip starts, and the out point determines where the clip ends.

SET IN AND OUT POINTS ON THE TIMELINE

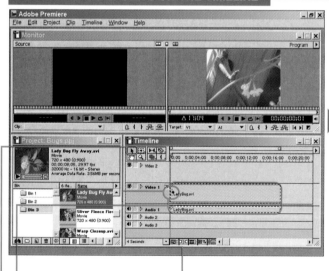

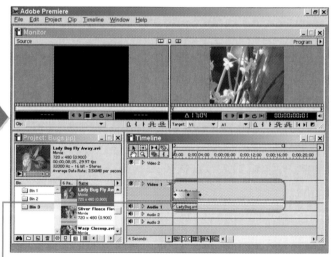

1 Click the clip you want to trim.

Note: See the section "Select a Clip in the Timeline" to select clips.

2 Click the **Selection** tool ( ).

3 Move the over the left edge of the clip (becomes).

4 Click and drag the in point to a new location on the track.

Which is the fastest method to trim a clip?

You can set in and out points in the Clip window, in Source view in the Monitor window, and in the Timeline window. Most editors find it easier to see how the in and out points affect frames in the clip using the Monitor window. See Chapter 7 to learn how to trim clips in the Monitor window.

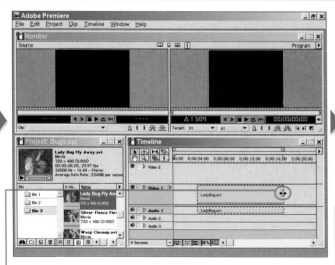

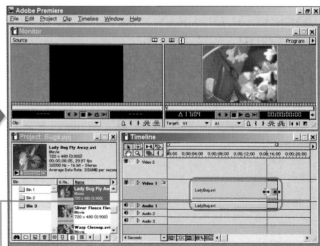

5 Move the ⌖ over the right edge of the clip (⌖ becomes ⬌).

6 Click and drag the out point to a new location on the track.

■ The new in and out points are set.

■ You can also click the In Point (⬛) and Out Point (⬛) tools in the toolbox to trim a clip in the Timeline.

CHANGE CLIP SPEED AND DURATION

You can change the speed of a clip to adjust the playback rate to play faster or slower. You can also change the length of time the clip plays, which yields the same result as changing the clip's in and out points.

See the section "Set In and Out Points on the Timeline" to learn another way to change clip duration.

CHANGE CLIP SPEED

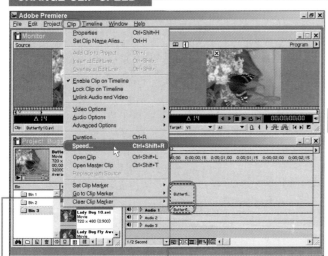

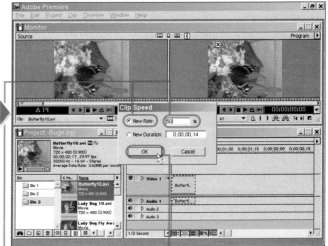

1 Click the clip you want to change.

2 Click **Clip**.

3 Click **Speed**.

■ The Clip Speed dialog box appears.

4 Click **New Rate** (○ changes to ◉).

5 Type a new speed rate based on a percentage of the normal speed.

■ A value greater than 100% increases the clip speed.

■ A value less than 100% decreases the clip speed.

■ A negative value makes the clip play in reverse.

6 Click **OK**.

■ The clip plays at the new speed when previewed.

**How do I change the speed of
a clip that is not yet in the
Timeline?**

Click the clip in the Project
window, click **Clip**, and then
click **Speed**. The Clip Speed
dialog box appears, enabling
you to adjust clip speed and
duration at the same time.

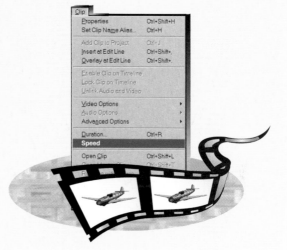

CHANGE CLIP DURATION

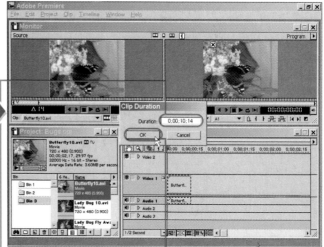

1 Click the clip you want to
change.

2 Click **Clip**.

3 Click **Duration**.

■ The Clip Duration dialog
box appears.

4 Type a new duration for
the clip.

■ A shorter duration
increases clip speed.

■ A longer duration
decreases clip speed.

5 Click **OK**.

■ The new duration is
assigned.

ADD PROGRAM MARKERS

You can use program markers to identify points in the Timeline. For example, you may add a program marker to identify where a title clip should begin or where a sound should start playing. Program markers are merely reference points that appear on the Timeline ruler. They do not appear in the final video project you output.

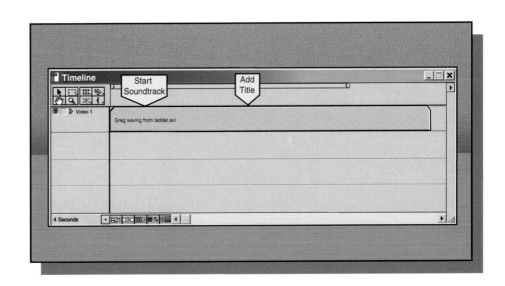

ADD PROGRAM MARKERS

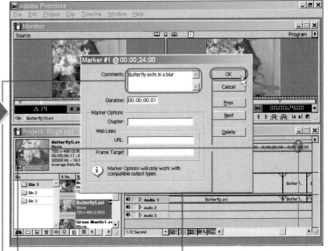

ADD A PROGRAM MARKER AND COMMENT

 Cue the Edit Line to where you want to add a marker.

Note: See Chapter 6 for information on navigating the Timeline window.

■2 Click **Timeline**.

■3 Click **Set Timeline Marker**.

■4 Click the type of marker you want to set.

■ The marker appears on the Timeline ruler.

■5 Double-click the marker.

■ The Marker dialog box appears.

■6 Type comment text.

■7 Click **OK**.

■ The comment is added to the marker.

■ To see the comment, hover the ⌖ over the marker.

160

How do I remove a marker I no longer need?

Locate the marker using the **Go to Timeline Marker** command. Then, click **Timeline**, **Clear Timeline Marker**, and finally **Current Marker**. Premiere removes the marker from the Timeline.

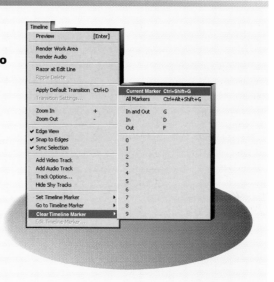

GO TO A MARKER

1 Click **Timeline**.

2 Click **Go to Timeline Marker**.

3 Click the type of marker you want to go to.

■ Premiere immediately scrolls to the marker location in the Timeline.

■ The marker icon appears on the Timeline ruler as well as above the program view in the Monitor window.

■ To view comment text, hover the mouse pointer over the marker.

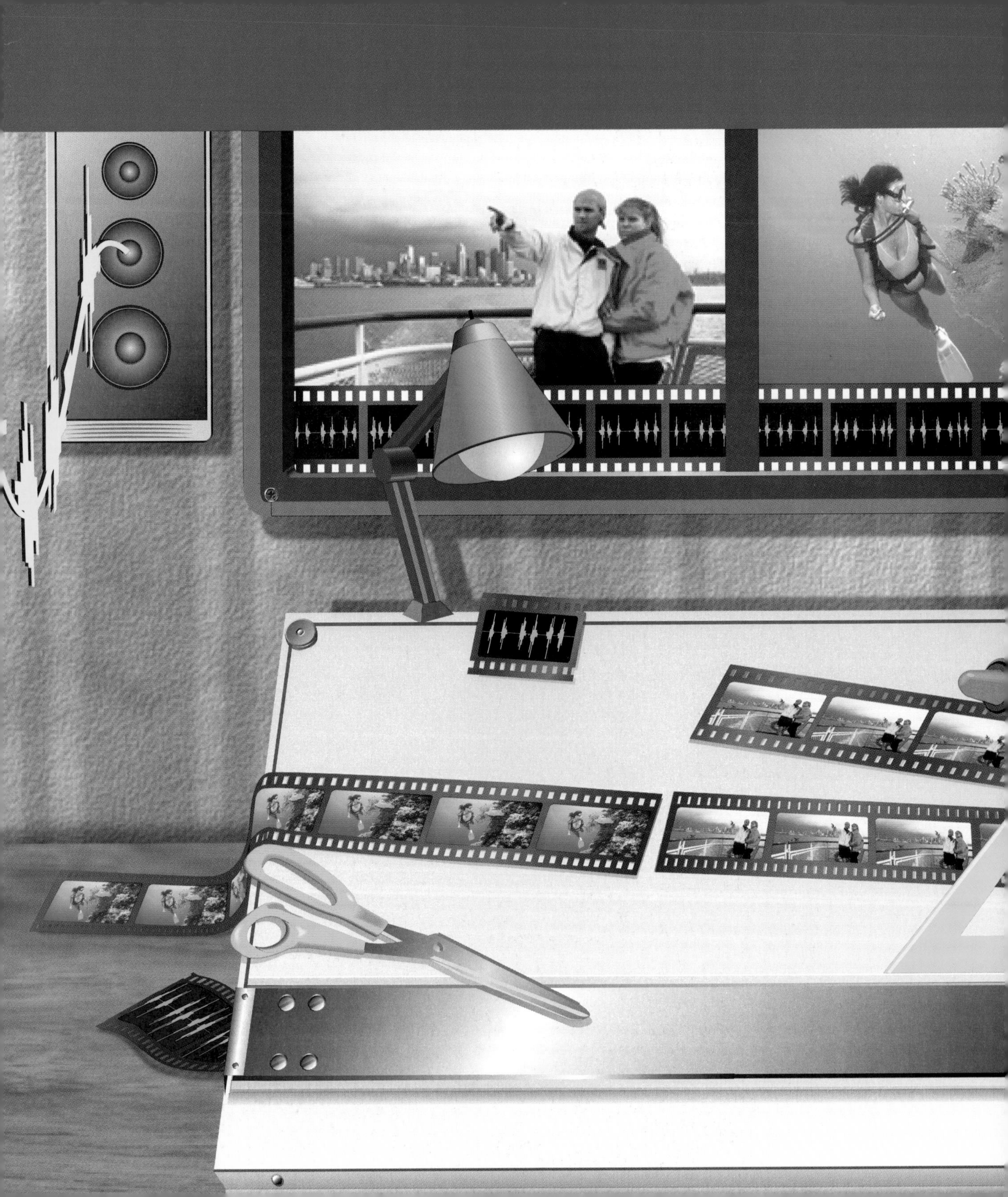

CHAPTER 9

Fine-Tuning a Program

Have you assembled your video? Does it need some fine-tuning? This chapter shows you helpful techniques editors use to polish and fine-tune a video program.

CREATE A RIPPLE EDIT

You can use a *ripple edit* to change the duration time of one clip without changing an adjacent clip. Rather than manually adjust the second clip to move over in the Timeline when you change the clip duration, the ripple edit moves the remaining clip for you to make sure that no gaps occur between the clips. Ripple edits affect the overall length of your video.

1 Click the clip you want to edit.

Note: Make sure the two clips are unlocked. See Chapter 8 to lock and unlock clips.

■ Note the clip duration and position before you edit.

■ In this example, the clip's original out point is displayed here.

2 Click the **Ripple Edit** tool (◆) (🖑 becomes ◆).

Note: See Chapter 8 to select toolbox tools.

My clip does not adjust when I click and drag an end point. Why not?

The clip is likely locked. You cannot edit locked clips or tracks in the Timeline window. See Chapter 6 to learn how to lock and unlock a track. See Chapter 8 to learn how to lock and unlock clips.

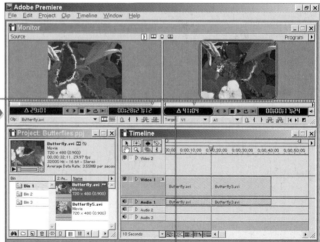

■ **3** Click and drag the in or out point of the clip you want to change.

■ To ripple edit an in point, click and drag the clip's in point icon.

■ To ripple edit an out point, click and drag the clip's out point icon.

■ The Program view shows how the edit affects both clips as you drag.

Note: See Chapter 6 to learn how to work with Timeline tracks.

■ The clip is edited and the remaining clip on the track shifts over to adjust for the change.

■ In this example, the first clip's out point is shortened, so the out point shows a new frame.

■ The overall project length is changed.

Note: See Chapter 7 to preview a video.

CREATE A ROLLING EDIT

You can use a rolling edit to change the out point of one clip and at the same time adjust the in point of the adjacent clip. A *rolling edit* enables you to shorten the current clip and make up the difference in program length by making the next clip longer.

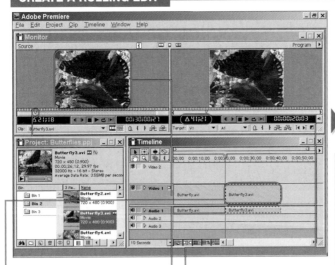

■1 Locate the clip you want to edit.

Note: Make sure the two clips are unlocked. See Chapter 8 to lock and unlock clips.

■ Note the program duration before you edit.

■ In this example, the clip's in point appears here.

■2 Click the **Rolling Edit** (▯▮▯) tool (▯ becomes ‡|‡).

Note: See Chapter 8 to view and select toolbox tools.

I am having trouble seeing the tracks in the Timeline window. Is there any way to zoom in to better see my edits?

You can make the tracks appear larger by customizing the Timeline window. Click **Window**, **Window Options**, and then **Timeline Window Options** to open the Timeline Window Options dialog box. Choose the largest icon size for the tracks and click **OK**. This should improve your view of the tracks.

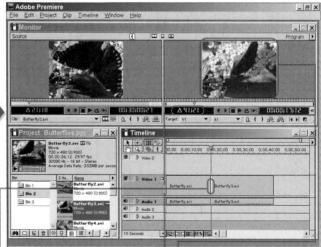

3 Click and drag the out point of the clip you want to change.

■ The Program view shows how the edit affects both clips as you drag.

Note: See Chapter 6 to learn how to work with Timeline tracks.

■ The out and in points are adjusted.

■ In this example, the second clip's in point was lengthened while the first clip's out point was shortened.

■ The second clip's new in point frame is displayed here.

■ No change occurred in program duration.

Note: See Chapter 7 to preview a video.

CREATE A SLIP EDIT

You can use a slip edit to move a clip's start and end frames without affecting adjacent clips. A *slip edit* essentially enables you to adjust a clip's in and out points without manually moving both points. The clip slips between frames without affecting the program length. A slip edit works only on clips that have frames beyond their in and out points and are among three adjacent clips.

CREATE A SLIP EDIT

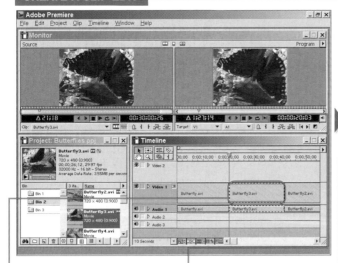

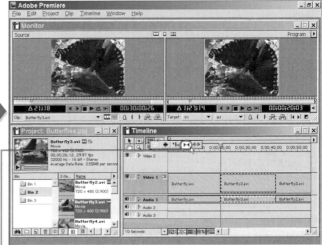

1 Click the clip you want to edit.

■ Note the program and clip duration before you edit.

■ In this example, the middle clip's in and out points appear here.

2 Click the **Slip Edit** tool (becomes ⊢⊣).

Note: See Chapter 8 to view and select toolbox tools.

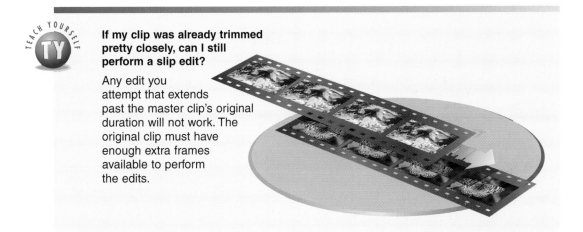

If my clip was already trimmed pretty closely, can I still perform a slip edit?

Any edit you attempt that extends past the master clip's original duration will not work. The original clip must have enough extra frames available to perform the edits.

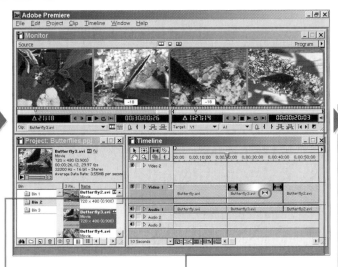

3 Click and drag the clip right or left to slip the clip's frames.

■ The Monitor window changes to show the frames at the edit points and the number of frames you slip or shift.

Note: See Chapter 8 to move clips on the Timeline.

■ The clip's new in and out points are set based on the number of frames you slip.

■ In this example, the clip's new in point frame appears here.

■ No change occurred in program or clip duration.

Note: See Chapter 7 to preview a video.

CREATE A SLIDE EDIT

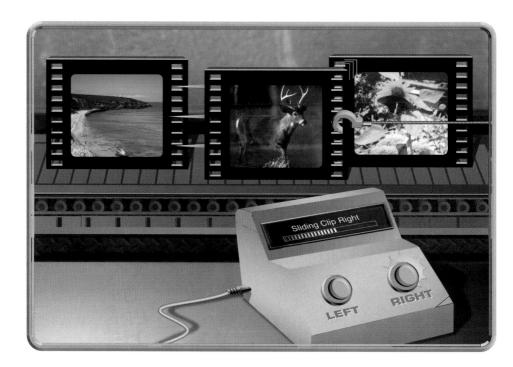

You can use a *slide edit* to maintain the current clip's duration while adjusting the adjacent clip's in and out points. If you slide the clip left, the out point of the clip to the left changes. If you slide the clip right, the in point of the clip to the right changes. The program length remains the same, and only the adjacent clips are affected. Premiere permits slide edits only if you have three clips side by side.

CREATE A SLIDE EDIT

1 Scroll to locate the clip you want to edit.

■ Note the program duration before you edit.

■ In this example, the first clip's out point appears here.

2 Click the **Slide Edit** tool (🖑 becomes ┣━┫).

Note: See Chapter 8 to view and select toolbox tools.

170

I do not like where I placed my slide edit. How do I undo the edit?

Click **Edit** and then **Undo** immediately after performing the edit. If the edit occurred several steps back, Premiere keeps track of your edits and lists them in the History palette. To display the palette, click **Window** and then **Show History**. When you click an edit in the list, Premiere undoes all edits performed after and including the selected edit.

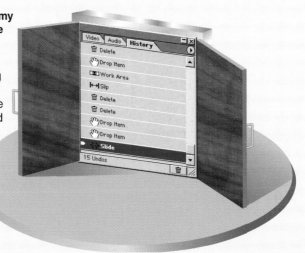

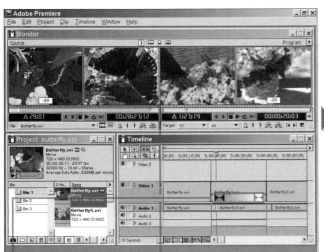

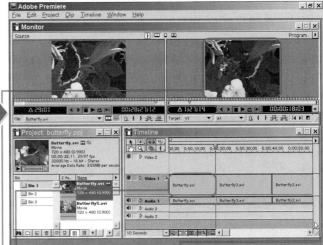

3 Click and drag the clip right or left to slide the adjacent clip's frames.

■ Drag the clip left to adjust the out point of the clip to the left.

■ Drag the clip right to adjust the in point of the clip to the right.

■ The Monitor window shows the frames at the edit points and the number of frames you slide or shift.

■ The adjacent clip's in and out points are changed.

■ In this example, the first clip's new out point frame appears here.

■ No change occurred in program duration.

Note: See Chapter 7 to preview a video.

EDIT IN TRIM MODE

You can use the Trim Mode view in the Monitor window to create detailed edits on your clips. Unlike editing in the Timeline window, Trim Mode enables you to see the current clip and the adjacent clip. You can see both sides of an edit between clips, which lets you view the frames affected by an edit.

1 Cue the **Edit Line** ( ) to the frame where you want to perform an edit.

Note: See Chapter 8 to cue the Edit Line in the Timeline window.

■ Optionally, to trim only the clips in selected tracks, select the tracks and click the **Toggle Shift Tracks** button ( ).

■ Optionally, click the **Toggle Sync Mode** button ( ) to trim both tracks for linked tracks you are editing.

Note: See Chapter 8 to learn how to work with the Timeline window.

How do I switch back to Dual or Single view?

After you finish trimming clips in Trim Mode view, click the **Dual View** (▭) or **Single View** (▭) button at the top of the Monitor window to switch back. You can also click the Timeline ruler in the Timeline window to switch back to the previous view.

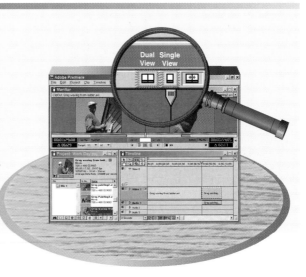

2 Click the **Trim Mode** button (▭).

■ The Monitor window switches to Trim Mode view.

Note: See Chapter 7 to learn how to work with Monitor window views.

3 Click ▾.

4 Click the video track you want to edit.

Note: To edit audio, click the ▾ labeled A1, A2, and so on, and click the audio track you want to edit.

■ You can now edit in Trim mode and view two adjacent clips.

Note: See "Perform a Ripple Edit in Trim Mode" and "Perform a Rolling Edit in Trim Mode" to learn more about using Trim Mode.

PERFORM A RIPPLE EDIT IN TRIM MODE

You can assign a *ripple edit* in Trim Mode view to change the duration of one clip without changing an adjacent clip. The ripple edit shifts the remaining clips over for you to make sure no gaps form between clips. By performing the ripple edit in Trim Mode view, you can see how the clip you are editing flows to the adjacent clip.

PERFORM A RIPPLE EDIT IN TRIM MODE

■1 Cue the **Edit Line** to where you want to perform an edit.

Note: See Chapter 8 to learn how to work with the Timeline window.

■2 Click the **Trim Mode** button (⬛).

■ The Monitor window switches to Trim Mode view.

■3 Click ▼ to specify target tracks.

Note: See the section "Edit in Trim Mode" to edit in Trim Mode view.

■4 Click a clip to edit.

■ Clicking the left image lets you edit the first clip's out point.

■ Clicking the right image lets you edit the second clip's in point.

■ The active image's display appears green.

■ You can also click the **Set Focus Left** (⬛) or **Set Focus Right** (⬛) buttons to specify which clip to edit.

174

Can I use a trim multiple other than 1 or 5?

Yes. You can customize the Trim Mode view to display another amount for trimming frames. For example, you may prefer to trim 3 frames at a time. Learn how to customize the Trim Mode view in the section "Customize Trim Mode."

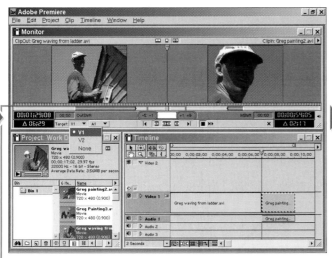

5 Click a trim button to trim the clip by the desired number of frames.

■ Clicking the **Trim Left** button (-1) trims one frame to the left.

■ Clicking the **Trim Right** button (+1) trims one frame to the right.

■ To trim frames in multiples of 5, click -5 or +5 .

■ You can also click and drag the in or out point to adjust the trim.

■ Clicking X cancels the edit and returns the clip to its previous state.

Note: See the section "Preview in Trim Mode" to preview a video.

PERFORM A ROLLING EDIT IN TRIM MODE

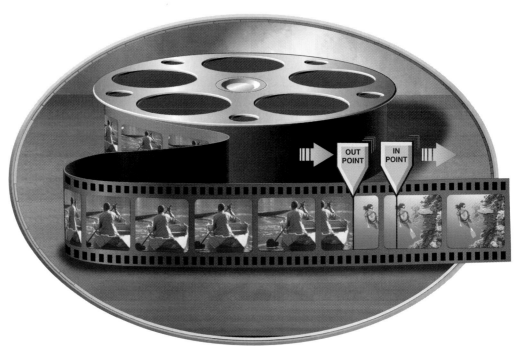

You can assign a rolling edit in Trim Mode view to simultaneously change clip's out point while adjusting the adjacent clip's in point. A *rolling edit* shortens one clip while lengthening another. By performing the rolling edit in Trim Mode view, you can see how the clip you are editing flows to the adjacent clip.

OUT POINT   IN POINT

PERFORM A ROLLING EDIT IN TRIM MODE

1 Cue the **Edit Line** where you want to perform an edit.

Note: See Chapter 8 to learn how to work with the Timeline window.

2 Click the **Trim Mode** button ().

■ The Monitor window switches to Trim Mode view.

3 Click ▼ to specify target tracks.

Note: See the section "Edit in Trim Mode" to prepare to edit in Trim Mode view.

4 Click the **Set Focus Both** button ( ).

■ Both views are selected, and the time readout displays appear green.

Can I type a precise number of frames for a rolling edit?

Yes. In the field between the two clips, type the number of frames you want to roll. Type a positive number to move right and a negative number to move left. Press `Enter` (Windows) or `Return` (Mac), and the edit is performed.

5 Click a trim button to trim the clips the desired number of frames.

■ Clicking the **Trim Left** button (`-1`) trims one frame to the left.

■ Clicking the **Trim Right** button (`+1`) trims one frame to the right.

■ To trim frames in multiples of 5, click `-5` or `+5` .

■ You can also click and drag the **Rolling Edit** pointer (🔖 becomes ⁝⁝⁝⁝ when the Set Focus Both button is selected) between the two clips to adjust the edit.

Note: See the section "Preview in Trim Mode" to preview a video.

PREVIEW AN EDIT IN TRIM MODE

After you assign an edit in Trim Mode view, you can preview the result in the Monitor window.

PREVIEW AN EDIT IN TRIM MODE

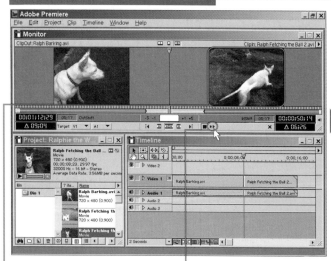

■1 Perform an edit in Trim Mode view.

Note: See the previous sections to edit in Trim Mode view.

■2 Click the **Play Edit** button (▶▶).

■ You can also press **Spacebar** to preview the edit.

■ The edit plays in the right side of the Monitor window.

CUSTOMIZE TRIM MODE

You can customize the
Trim Mode view in the
Monitor window by
changing how frames
are displayed and by
indicating the number
of multiple frames
that are edited.

CUSTOMIZE TRIM MODE

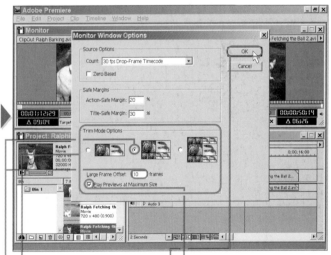

1 With Trim Mode
displayed, click **Window**.

*Note: See Chapter 7 to learn how to
use Monitor window views.*

2 Click **Window Options**.

3 Click **Monitor Window
Options**.

■ The Monitor Window
Options dialog box appears.

4 Make changes among
the Trim Mode Options.

■ Clicking display options
controls how frames display
(○ changes to ◉).

■ You can type a number to
specify a larger or smaller
multiple frame option for
incremental edits.

■ Clicking this option
ensures that the preview
plays at the maximum size
(☐ changes to ☑).

5 Click **OK**.

■ The new settings take
effect.

PERFORM A SPLIT EDIT IN THE TIMELINE

You can perform a split edit, also called an *L-cut*, to make a clip's audio track synchronize with another clip. The most common use for this type of edit is to show someone talking and then show another person but still hear the first person talking. You can perform a split edit in the Timeline to see how much of the audio clip shifts between two video clips.

PERFORM A SPLIT EDIT IN THE TIMELINE

1 Cue the **Edit Line** to where you want to create a split edit.

2 Click the **Toggle Sync Mode** button (🖳) to toggle the mode off.

■ 🖳 indicates the mode is off.

3 Click the **Rolling Edit** button (✦) (▷ becomes ‡|‡).

What is a J-cut?

A *J-cut* occurs when the audio in point appears earlier than the video in point. An *L-cut*, on the other hand, is the reverse — an audio in point appears after the video in point.

4 Click and drag the out point of the audio clip to create an L-cut on the Timeline.

Note: See Chapter 6 to learn how to work with Timeline tracks.

5 Click the **Toggle Sync Mode** button (☰) to toggle the mode back on again.

■ 8☰ indicates the mode is on.

■ You can now preview the edit in the Monitor window.

Note: See Chapter 7 to preview a video.

PERFORM A SPLIT EDIT IN TRIM MODE

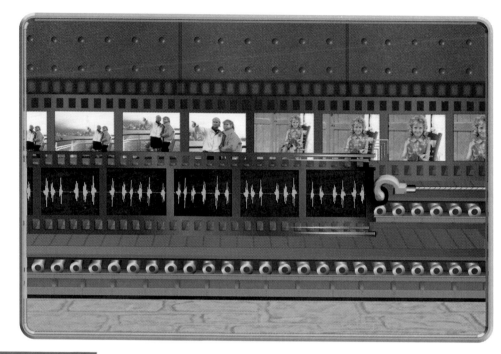

You can perform a split edit, also called an *L-cut*, in Trim Mode view to make a clip's audio track synchronize with another clip. For example, you may show a clip of someone talking and then show another person but still hear the first person talking. A split edit is a great way to make the video more interesting.

PERFORM A SPLIT EDIT IN TRIM MODE

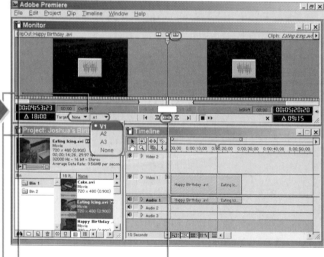

1 Cue the **Edit Line** to where you want to create a split edit.

2 Click the **Toggle Sync Mode** button (🔳) to toggle the mode off.

■ 🔳 indicates the mode is off.

3 Click the **Trim Mode** button (🔳).

■ The Monitor window switches to Trim Mode view.

4 Click 🔽 to specify target tracks.

Note: See "Edit in Trim Mode" to edit in Trim Mode view.

5 Click the **Set Focus Both** button (🔳).

■ Both views are selected.

Can I make the audio track cross-fade?

Yes. A cross-fade is a good effect to apply to an audio clip that is used for a split edit. To learn how to cross-fade an audio clip, see Chapter 10.

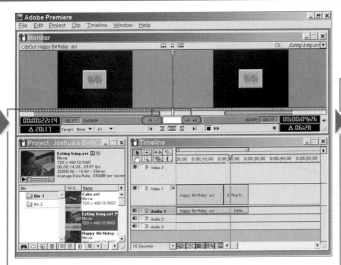

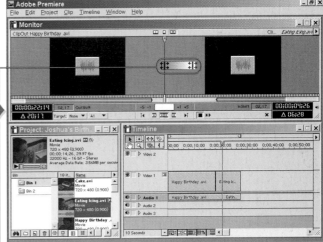

6 Click a trim button to trim the clips the desired number of frames.

■ Clicking the **Trim Left** button (-1) trims one frame to the left.

■ Clicking the **Trim Right** button (+1) trims one frame to the right.

■ To trim frames in multiples of 5, click -5 or +5 .

■ You can also click and drag the **Rolling Edit** pointer (becomes) when the Set Focus Both button is selected) between the two clips to adjust the edit.

■ The number of trimmed frames for each clip appears here.

Note: See "Preview an Edit in Trim Mode" to preview a split edit.

CHAPTER 10

Editing Audio

Would your video project benefit from some sound? This chapter shows you how to work with audio files and mix audio clips.

UNDERSTANDING VIDEO SOUND

Sound, or audio, is an important part of any project. It can help set the mood of your project and enhance the impact of your video images. You can use up to 99 audio tracks in your Premiere video project. You can adjust the *audio level,* or volume, of each sound to get just the right overall mix.

Where Can I Find Sound Clips?

All sounds you incorporate into Premiere must be digitized. You can import sound clips, such as AIF, MP3, and WAV file types. See Chapter 4 to learn how to import files. You can also use the sounds recorded along with video footage shot with a recording device, such as a MiniDV camcorder.

Audio Tracks

You can use audio tracks, which are located directly below the video tracks in the Timeline window, to assemble sound clips or sounds recorded along with the video footage. By default, Premiere provides three audio tracks to every new project. You can add additional audio tracks as needed.

Working with Sound Clips

Sound clips work in much the same way as video clips. You can open a sound clip in a Clip window, but rather than viewing a visual image, you see the sound's waveform pattern. From within the Clip window, you can play the clip, determine where a clip starts and ends, and more.

Gaining and Fading Sound

The most popular ways to edit sound is to control the gain, or volume, or to fade sound in and out. The Gain command enables you to adjust an entire audio clip's volume. Premiere's fade controls enable you to gradually fade sound in or out for a particular clip.

Balancing Volume

You can control the balance of sound between the left and right speakers by using Premiere's panning controls. For example, if your video image shows a truck driving by from left to right, you can pan the truck's sound so it moves from the left speaker to the right speaker to correspond.

Mixing Audio

You can open the Audio Mixer window to mix sound for one or several clips at once. The Audio Mixer looks very much like a traditional mixing board with stylized controls, such as pan knobs and faders, for mixing sounds on tracks.

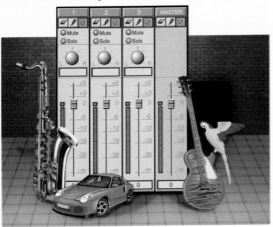

Using Audio Effects

Premiere provides audio effects that you can apply to correct and enhance your video's sounds. The Audio Effects palette contains 20 audio effects, such as Boost, Chorus, Echo, and Reverb. After you apply an audio effect, you can adjust the effect to suit your needs.

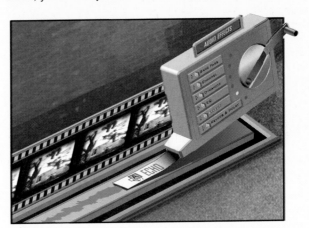

VIEW AUDIO CONTROLS

You can view the audio controls for an individual audio track in the Timeline window to quickly access pan and fade lines for making adjustments to the clip volume. All tracks in the timeline expand or collapse. Only in the expanded state are controls visible.

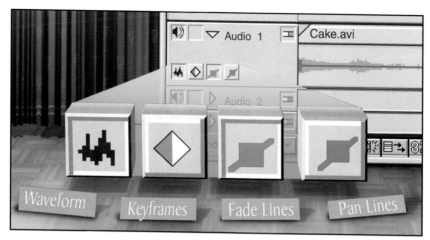

The *pan line* controls the balance of audio between the left and right speakers. The *fade line* controls the volume level.

VIEW AUDIO CONTROLS

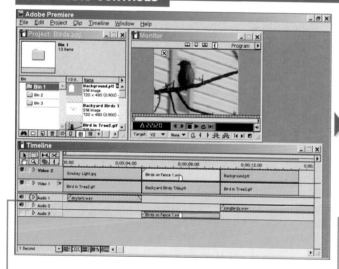

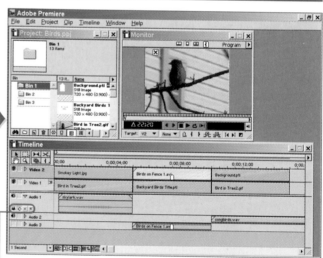

1 With a project open, click the audio track's **Expand** (▷) icon.

■ Premiere expands the track.

Note: See Chapter 6 to learn more about working with tracks in the timeline.

2 Click a control.

■ Clicking 🐦 toggles between a visible and hidden waveform in the track.

■ Clicking ◇ toggles between visible and hidden keyframes for audio effects you assign.

■ Clicking ▨ toggles between a visible and hidden fade line.

■ Clicking ▨ toggles between a visible and hidden pan line.

PLAY AN AUDIO CLIP

You can open the Clip
window to play an audio
clip. The Clip window
has controls for playing,
looping, setting in and
out points that determine
where a clip starts and
ends, and more.

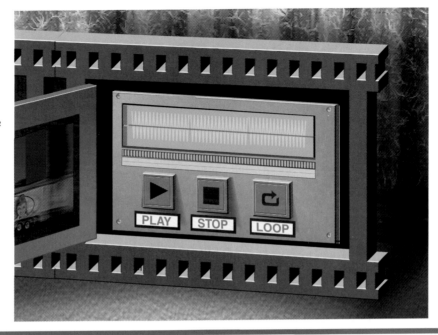

PLAY AN AUDIO CLIP

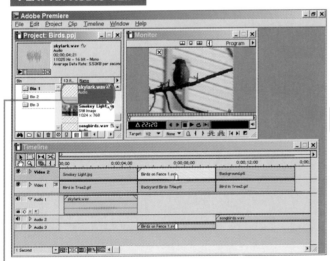

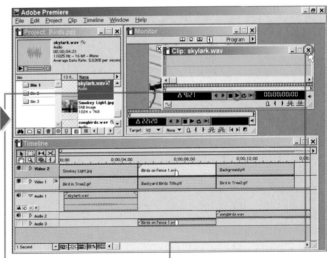

1 With a project open,
double-click the audio clip
in the Project window.

■ The Clip window opens.

*Note: You can also play a sound clip
in the Project window by clicking the
Play button (▶).*

2 Click ▶ to play the clip.

■ Clicking ◀ and ▶ moves
the Set Location Line back
and forth a frame.

■ Clicking ■ stops the play.

■ Clicking ↻ causes the
clip to loop during play.

3 Click ✕ (Windows) or
□ (Mac) to close the Clip
window.

*Note: See Chapter 5 to learn how to
set in and out points.*

ADD AN AUDIO CLIP TO THE TIMELINE

You can add audio clips to the audio tracks in the Timeline window in the same way in which video clips are added.

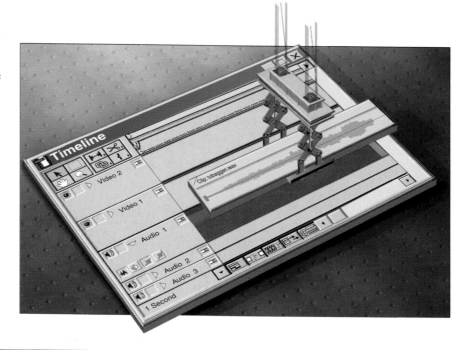

ADD AN AUDIO CLIP TO THE TIMELINE

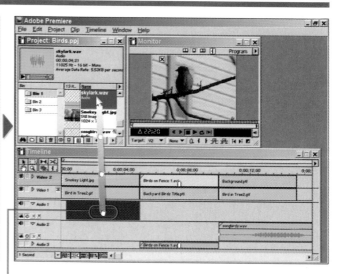

1 With a project open, locate the sound clip you want to add to the Timeline.

Note: See Chapter 4 to learn how to import production elements into Premiere.

2 Drag and drop the clip onto an audio track (➤ becomes 🖑).

■ The clip appears in the track.

Note: See Chapter 6 to learn more about working with Timeline tracks.

■ To play the video in the Monitor window, save the project and then press **Enter** (Windows) or **Return** (Mac).

Note: See Chapter 2 to save a project, and Chapter 5 to set in and out points.

190

CHANGE VOLUME WITH THE GAIN COMMAND

You can adjust the
volume for an entire
audio clip using the
Gain command. You
can raise or lower the
volume, depending on
your needs.

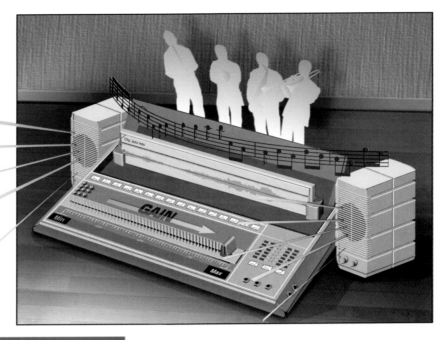

CHANGE VOLUME WITH THE GAIN COMMAND

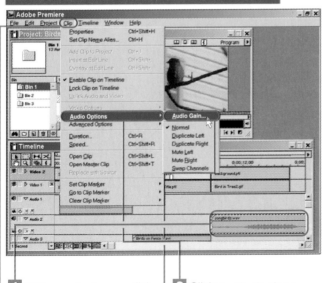

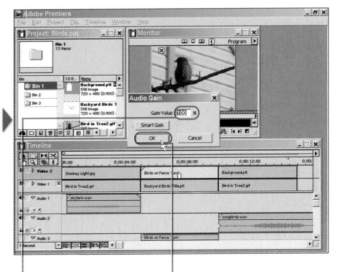

1 With a project open, click
the audio clip you want to
adjust.

2 Click **Clip**.

3 Click **Audio Options**.

4 Click **Audio Gain**.

■ The Audio Gain dialog
box appears.

5 Type a value based on
percentage of volume.

■ Type a number greater
than 100% to increase
volume.

■ Type a number less than
100% to decrease volume.

6 Click **OK**.

■ To hear the sound clip,
press **Enter** (Windows) or
Return (Mac).

FADE A SOUND

You can use a track's *fade line*, also called the rubberband option, to fade a sound in or out during a clip. For example, you may want a sound to gradually increase in volume or to fade out at the end of the clip. Using the fade line, which appears red in the audio track, you can control the clip's audio level.

Clip: motorcycle.wav

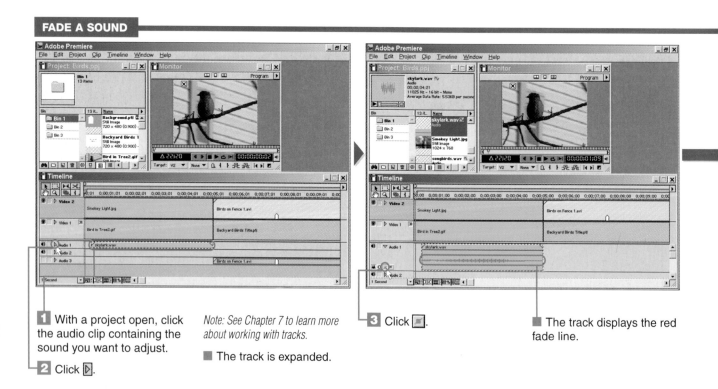

1 With a project open, click the audio clip containing the sound you want to adjust.

2 Click ▷.

Note: See Chapter 7 to learn more about working with tracks.

■ The track is expanded.

3 Click ▣.

■ The track displays the red fade line.

What are the limits to the audio level I can fade?

By default, Premiere starts a sound clip at 100%. You can drag the fade line up to 200%, which is twice the volume, or drag the fade line to 0%, which is no sound.

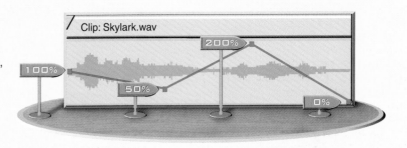

■ **4** Click and drag the left or right fade handle up or down to increase or decrease the audio level.

■ The volume increases as you drag the handle higher.

■ To gradually fade the sound out, move the right end of the fade line down at the end of the clip.

■ **5** Press **Enter** (Windows) or **Return** (Mac).

■ Premiere previews the sound in the Monitor window.

■ Click the fade line to add another fade handle that you can move or adjust.

■ To remove a fade handle, click and drag it outside the audio track.

USING THE FADE SCISSORS TOOL

You can use the Fade
Scissors tool to help
you make further
adjustments to a clip's
fade line. The Fade
Scissors tool enables
you to "cut" the fade
line by inserting two
adjustable side-by-side
fade handles. The Fade
Scissors tool is part of
the Timeline window's
toolbox.

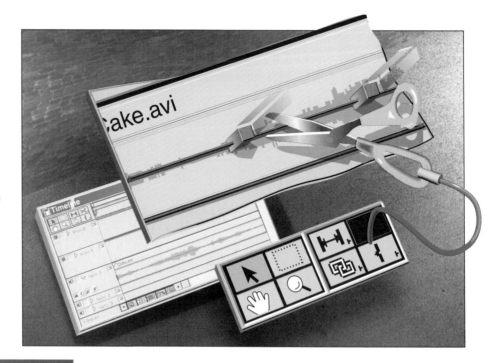

USING THE FADE SCISSORS TOOL

1 With a project open, click
the audio clip containing the
sound you want to adjust.

2 Click ▷.

*Note: See Chapter 7 to learn more
about working with tracks.*

■ The track is expanded.

3 Click ▣.

■ The track displays the red
fade line.

4 Click the **Fade Scissors**
tool (✂.) (▷ becomes ✄).

*Note: If the Fade Scissors tool is not
showing, click ✂ and then press
C on the keyboard to cycle through
the buttons until you see the Fade
Scissors button.*

How do I use the Fade Adjustment tool to edit the audio fade line?

When you use the Fade Adjustment tool (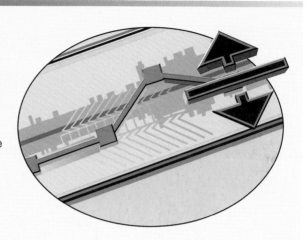), you can click and drag the fade line to move it at a constant percentage. In other words, any handles on the fade line move as a single line.

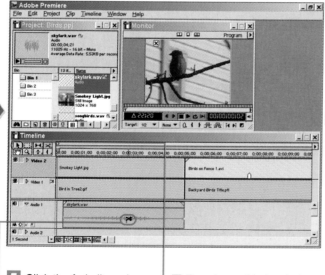

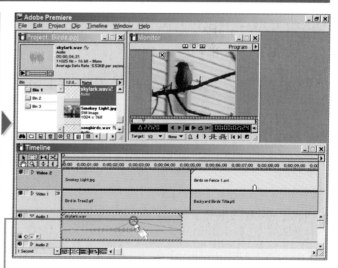

5 Click the fade line where you want to add fade handles to the sound (becomes ✖).

■ Premiere adds two fade handles, one right next to the other.

6 Click the **Selection** tool (▶).

7 Click and drag a fade handle to adjust the fade point.

8 Press **Enter** (Windows) or **Return** (Mac).

■ Premiere previews the sound in the Monitor window.

CREATE A CROSS FADE

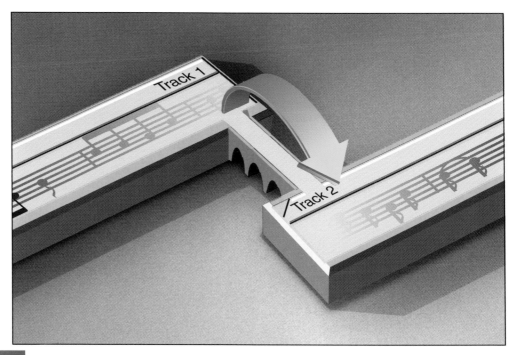

You can create a *cross fade*, the process of one sound clip fading out while another sound clip fades in. To perform a cross fade, the two sound clips must overlap in the Timeline window.

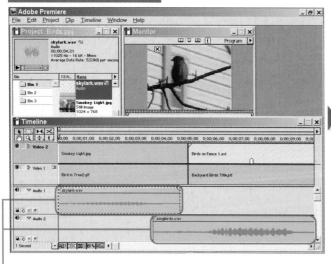

1 With a project open, add two overlapping sound clips.

Note: See "Add a Clip to the Timeline" to add sound clips to audio tracks.

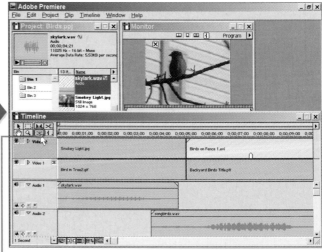

2 Click the **Cross Fade** tool (⊠).

Note: If the Cross Fade tool is not showing, click ⬍ , and then press U on the keyboard to cycle through the buttons until you see ⊠ .

How do I create a cross fade effect for a sound recorded with my video footage?

To turn the audio portion of the recording into a separate sound clip, click the clip in the Timeline, click **Clip**, and then click **Unlink Audio and Video**. Premiere immediately unlinks the two clips and marks both clips with a white link icon. You can now move and edit the audio as a separate sound clip.

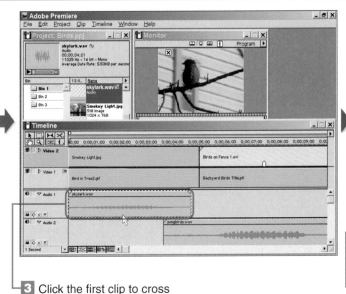

3 Click the first clip to cross fade.

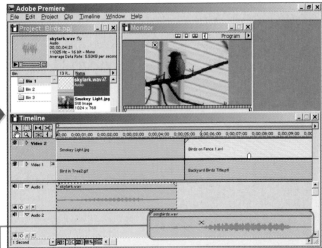

4 Click the second clip to cross fade (changes to ▷◁).

■ A standard cross fade effect is created.

5 Press Enter (Windows) or Return (Mac).

■ Premiere previews the sound in the Monitor window.

PAN A CLIP

You can control the balance of sound in an audio clip by panning the clip. Panning enables you to make the sound move from the left speaker to the right, right to left, or both. For example, your video may show a person walking along a sidewalk. With panning, you can make the footstep sounds seem to follow the person based on the direction they enter and exit the frame.

PAN A CLIP

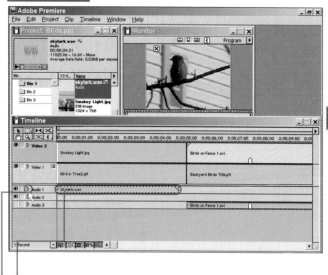

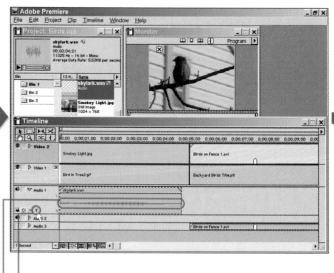

1 With a project open, click the audio clip containing the sound you want to adjust.

2 Click ▷.

Note: See Chapter 7 to learn more about working with tracks.

■ The track is expanded.

3 Click 🖪.

■ The track displays a blue line, also called the pan line.

Note: By default, Premiere sets the pan line so that both left and right speaker sounds are audible.

Can I use the Fade Adjustment and Fade Scissors tools on keyframes on the pan line?

Yes. The tools are interchangeable with the video fade line as well as the audio fade and pan lines. See the section "Using the Fade Scissors Tool" to learn more. To learn more about the tools found in the Timeline window's toolbox, see Chapter 7.

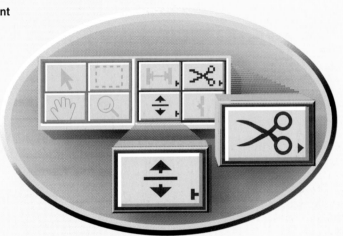

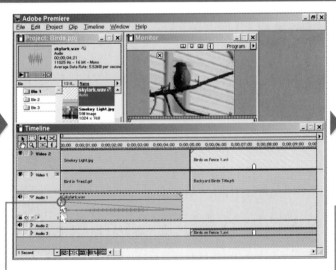

■ **4** Click and drag the left or right pan handle up or down to designate sound direction.

■ Move the pan line up to make audio play through the left speaker.

■ Move the pan line down to make audio play through the right speaker.

■ To make adjustments to sound direction along the pan line, click the line to add additional handles to control.

■ **5** Press **Enter** (Windows) or **Return** (Mac).

■ Premiere previews the sound in the Monitor window.

■ To remove a handle, click and drag it outside the audio track.

USING THE AUDIO MIXER

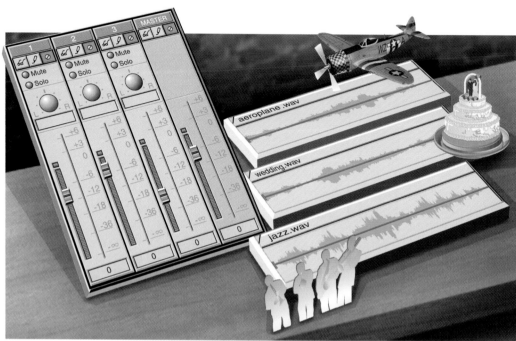

You can use the Audio Mixer window to mix volume and balance, also called *gain* and *pan,* of a single clip or several clips. For example, you can create pans using the pan knobs, or you can adjust the fader to create a fade effect. The Audio Mixer opens showing the number of active audio tracks in the Timeline window.

USING THE AUDIO MIXER

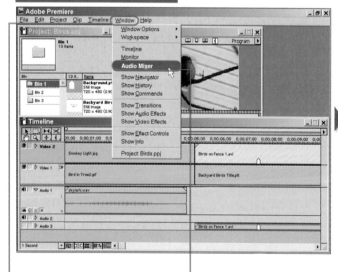

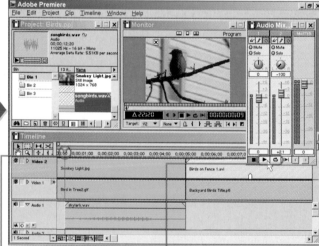

■1 With a project open, click **Window**.

■2 Click **Audio Mixer**.

■ The Audio Mixer window opens.

■3 Cue the edit line in the Timeline window to the spot where you want to start mixing.

Note: See Chapter 5 to learn how to cue the edit line.

■4 Click ▶ or ↻.

■ Premiere plays the audio.

My program window is pretty crowded. Is there a better way to edit audio in my current workspace?

Premiere has a preconfigured editing workspace you can use to help you edit audio content in your project. Click **Window**, **Workspace**, and then **Audio** to optimize the workspace for mixing audio. See Chapter 2 to learn more about Premiere workspace settings.

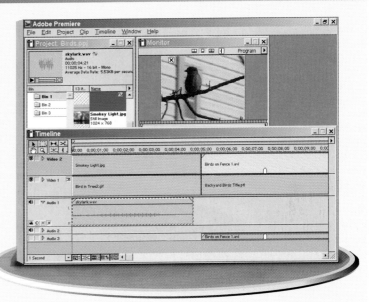

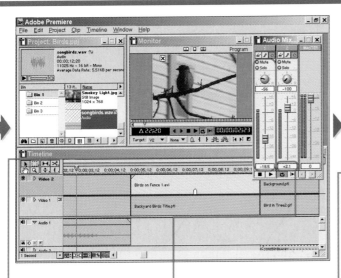

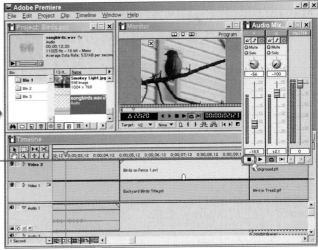

5 Adjust the Audio Mixer controls as needed.

■ Click and drag the **Volume** fader (≣) to fade a track's audio.

■ Click the **Pan/Balance** knob (◔) to pan the track's audio.

■ You can also type a value in the Pan/Balance or Volume fader fields.

6 Click ■ to stop mixing.

■ Any adjustments you made are added to the audio tracks.

APPLY AN AUDIO EFFECT

You can apply audio effects, also called *filters*, to your project for added enhancement or audio correction. You can add as many effects as you like to a sound clip. Premiere provides 20 different audio effects in the Audio Effects palette.

See Chapter 1 to learn more about using Premiere palettes.

APPLY THE AUDIO EFFECT

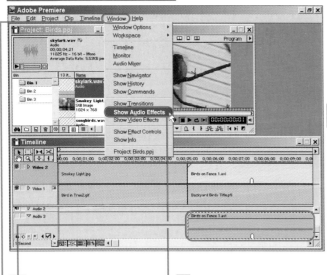

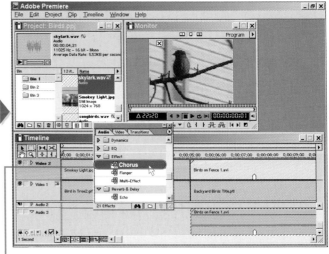

1 With a project open, click the sound clip to which you want to assign an effect.

2 Click **Window**.

3 Click **Show Audio Effects**.

■ The Audio Effects palette opens.

4 Click the effect you want to use.

■ Clicking ▶ opens a folder and lists associated effects.

■ Clicking ▽ closes a folder list.

■ Clicking ✕ or ☐ closes the palette entirely.

■ Clicking the scroll bar lets you view all the available folders and effects.

How can I edit audio effects?

You can edit audio effects listed in the Effect Controls palette, or you can open an effect's Settings dialog box and make adjustments to the effect's parameters. To open the Effect Controls palette, click **Window**, and then click **Show Effect Controls**. To learn more about editing effects with this palette, see Chapter 13.

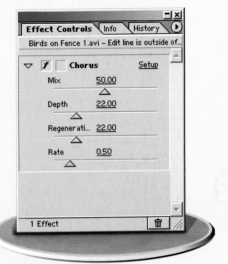

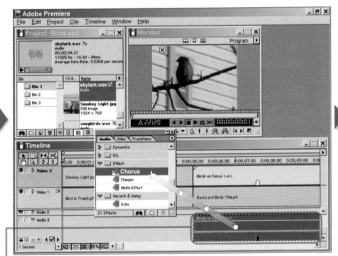

5 Drag the effect from the palette and drop it on the clip (🖑 becomes 🖐).

■ The effect is added to the clip, and the Effect Controls palette appears.

Note: Each effect you assign appears in the Effect Controls palette list.

■ To preview the effect, press **Enter** (Windows) or **Return** (Mac).

■ You can use the Effect Controls panel to adjust the effect's parameters.

Note: See Chapter 13 to fine-tune effects.

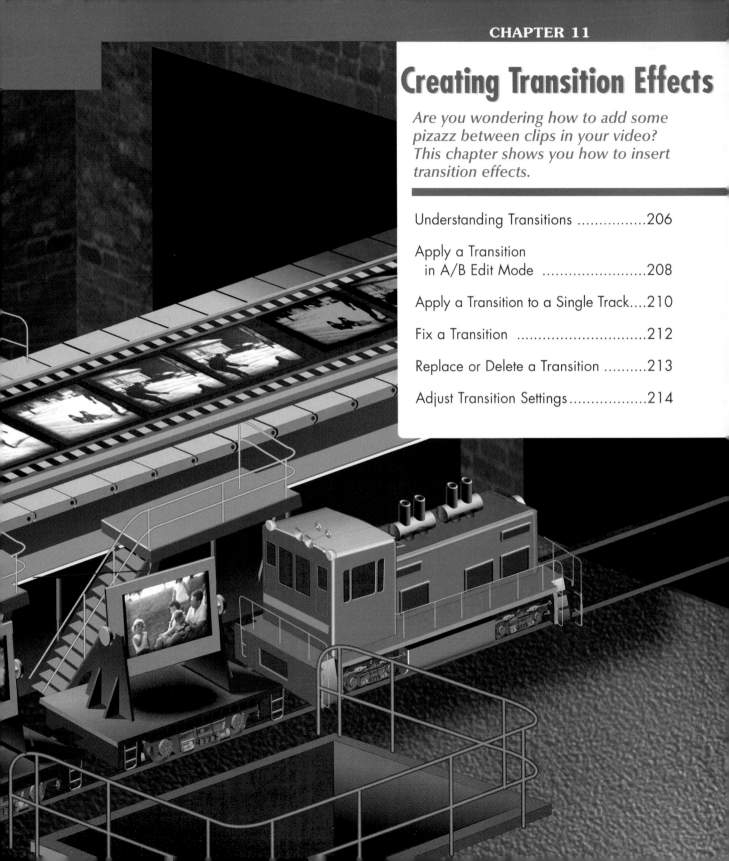

CHAPTER 11

Creating Transition Effects

Are you wondering how to add some pizazz between clips in your video? This chapter shows you how to insert transition effects.

LUNDERSTANDING TRANSITIONS

You can assign transitions to your video that help segue from one clip to another. Premiere offers more than 75 transition effects that you can apply and customize to meet your project's needs.

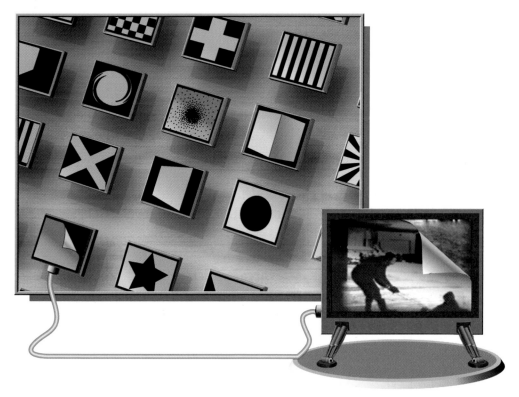

What are Transitions?

A *transition* is simply an effect you can apply that controls how one clip visually replaces the next clip in the video. Transitions can be as simple as a wipe from left to right, or as complex as a spiraling effect in which the next clip seems to spiral out from the center of the screen.

Why Use Transitions?

Transitions are great for showing the passage of time between two clips or moving from one scene to an entirely new scene. Transitions can add drama or create a bridge between clips.

Using the Transitions Palette

You can find plenty of transitions to choose from in the Transitions palette. Transitions are organized in folders. You can open a folder to display a list of associated transitions, and expand or collapse folders as needed. To learn more about using Premiere's palettes, see Chapter 1.

A/B Edit Mode

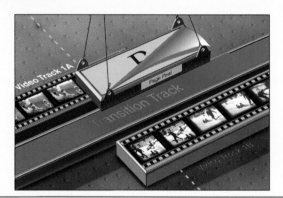

When you apply a transition in A/B edit mode, you place the transition on the Transition track. You must have one clip in Video Track 1A and another clip in Video Track 1B, and both clips must overlap to create the transition effect.

Single-Track Transitions

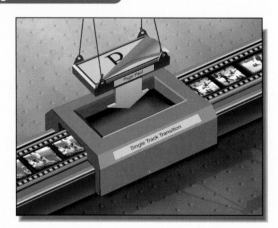

When you apply a transition in Single-Track edit mode, you insert the transition between two clips on a single track. For the transition to work, there must be enough extra frames between the two clips. The first clip must have extra frames at the out point and the second clip must have extra frames at the in point. To learn more about setting in and out points, see Chapter 7.

APPLY A TRANSITION IN A/B EDIT MODE

You can insert a transition in A/B edit mode using the Transition track. As long as a clip in Video Track 1A overlaps a clip in Video Track 1B, you can position a transition between the two. The overlap determines the transition's duration.

See Chapter 2 to learn more about editing modes.

APPLY A TRANSITION IN A/B EDIT MODE

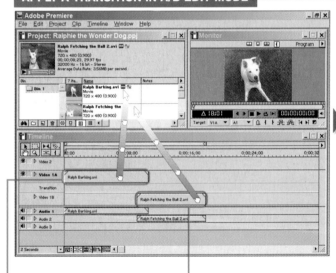

1 Drag a clip from the Project window and drop it into Video Track 1A.

2 Drag another clip from the Project window and drop it into Video Track 1B, overlapping a few frames.

Note: See Chapter 6 to learn more about working in the Timeline window.

3 Click **Window**.

4 Click **Show Transitions**.

■ The Transitions palette appears.

Note: See Chapter 1 to learn more about working with Premiere palettes.

How do I adjust a transition after it is in place?

You can click the transition and drag it on the Transition track, or you can click and drag an edge of the transition to make it longer or shorter. If you move a transition's edge, the edge of the clip may move as well. To control this, press Ctrl (Windows) or ⌘ (Mac) while dragging an edge.

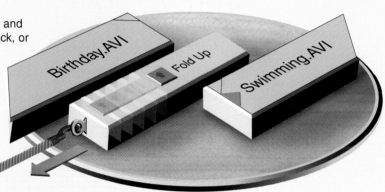

5 Locate the transition you want to use.

Note: To preview a transition, double-click it to open its Settings dialog box and view the effect.

6 Drag the transition from the palette and drop it into the Transition track between the two overlapping clips.

■ The transition appears on the track.

7 Save the project.

Note: See Chapter 2 to save a project.

8 Press Enter (Windows) or Return (Mac).

*Note: You can also click **Preview** from the **Timeline** menu to preview the video.*

■ Premiere builds a preview, and then the video plays in the Monitor window, showing any transitions assigned.

APPLY A TRANSITION TO A SINGLE TRACK

If you are editing your project in Single-Track edit mode, you can insert a transition between two clips on a single track. The clips you use must include extra frames that go beyond the out and in points. Premiere uses the extra frames to create the transition.

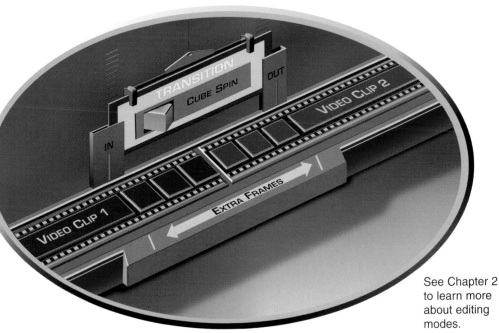

See Chapter 2 to learn more about editing modes.

APPLY A TRANSITION TO A SINGLE TRACK

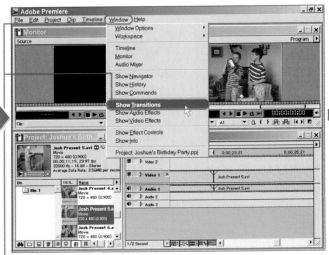

1 Drag and drop a clip onto a video track.

Note: See Chapter 6 to learn more about working in the Timeline window.

2 Drag and drop another clip to the same video track following the first clip.

Note: The first clip should have extra frames at the out point, and the second clip should have extra frames at the in point.

3 Click **Window**.

4 Click **Show Transitions**.

■ The Transitions palette appears.

Note: See Chapter 1 to learn more about working with Premiere palettes.

How many extra frames should a clip have?

A transition in Single-Track edit mode is determined by the number of extra frames at the beginning or end of the clips. To create a 30-frame dissolve transition between two clips, for example, each clip should have 15 extra frames. The first clip needs 15 extra frames at the out point and the second clip needs 15 extra frames at the in point. See Chapter 7 to learn how to create in and out points.

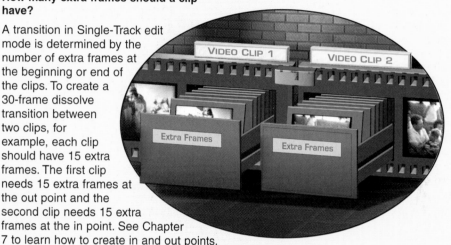

5 Locate the transition you want to use.

Note: To preview a transition, double-click it to open the transition's Settings dialog box and view the effect.

6 Drag and drop the transition in between the two clips.

Note: If there is an insufficient number of frames between the two clips to create the transition, the Fix Transition dialog box opens. See "Fix a Transition" to learn more.

■ The transition appears on the track.

7 Save the project.

Note: See Chapter 2 to save a project.

8 Press Enter (Windows) or Return (Mac).

*Note: You can also click **Preview** from the **Timeline** menu to preview the video.*

■ Premiere previews the transition in the Monitor window.

■ Click here to split the track and view the Transition track separately.

FIX A TRANSITION

You can add a transition between clips in Single-Track edit mode, but if you do not have enough extra frames to create the effect, Premiere prompts you to fix the transition. To fix the effect, you can change the clip duration or repeat frames.

See Chapter 2 to learn more about editing modes.

FIX A TRANSITION

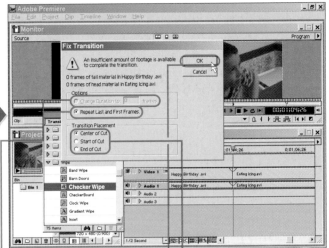

1 Add a transition between two clips in Single-Track edit mode.

Note: See the section "Add a Transition to a Single Track."

■ If there are not enough frames to apply a transition, the Fix Transition dialog box appears.

2 Select changes to fix the transition (○ changes to ◉).

■ Click here to shorten the duration of the transition effect and specify the number of frames.

■ Click here to repeat the frames to make up the difference.

■ Click one of these settings to change the transition's alignment.

3 Click **OK**.

■ Premiere adjusts the transition accordingly.

You can swap one transition for another, or you can delete an entire transition. When you remove a transition, the video plays with cuts from one clip to another rather than the transition effect.

REPLACE OR DELETE A TRANSITION

REPLACE A TRANSITION

1 Click the transition.

Note: See the sections "Apply a Transition in A/B Edit Mode" or "Add a Transition to a Single Track" to insert transitions.

2 Drag a new transition over the selected transition.

■ Premiere swaps the current transition with the new transition.

DELETE A TRANSITION

1 Click the transition.

2 Press the Delete key on your keyboard.

■ The transition disappears from the track.

ADJUST TRANSITION SETTINGS

You can customize a transition for even greater control. For example, you may change the way it appears during playback or change the track direction. Depending on the transition, you may select additional options to customize the effect, such as color or point of origin.

ADJUST TRANSITION SETTINGS

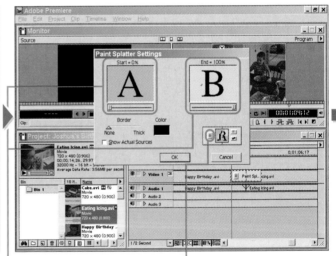

1 Double-click the transition you want to customize.

Note: See the sections "Apply a Transition in A/B Edit Mode" or "Add a Transition to a Single Track" to add transitions.

■ You can click here to reverse the transition direction.

■ The transition's Settings dialog box opens.

Note: The options available vary by transition.

2 Adjust the transition settings as needed.

■ The left icon represents the transition's start point.

■ The right icon represents the transition's end point.

■ To switch the start and end points, click here. This changes the direction of the transition.

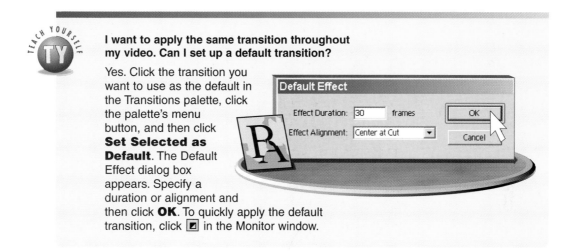

I want to apply the same transition throughout my video. Can I set up a default transition?

Yes. Click the transition you want to use as the default in the Transitions palette, click the palette's menu button, and then click **Set Selected as Default**. The Default Effect dialog box appears. Specify a duration or alignment and then click **OK**. To quickly apply the default transition, click 🔲 in the Monitor window.

Default Effect

Effect Duration: 30 frames

Effect Alignment: Center at Cut

OK
Cancel

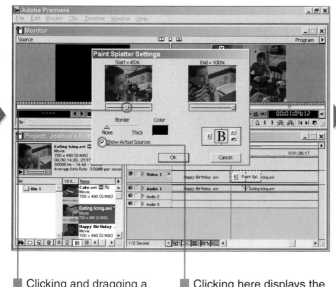

■ Clicking and dragging a slider changes where the transition effect starts.

■ Clicking here displays the actual clips involved with the transition (☐ changes to ☑).

3 When you have changed the settings to the way you want them, click **OK**.

■ Premiere applies the new settings.

215

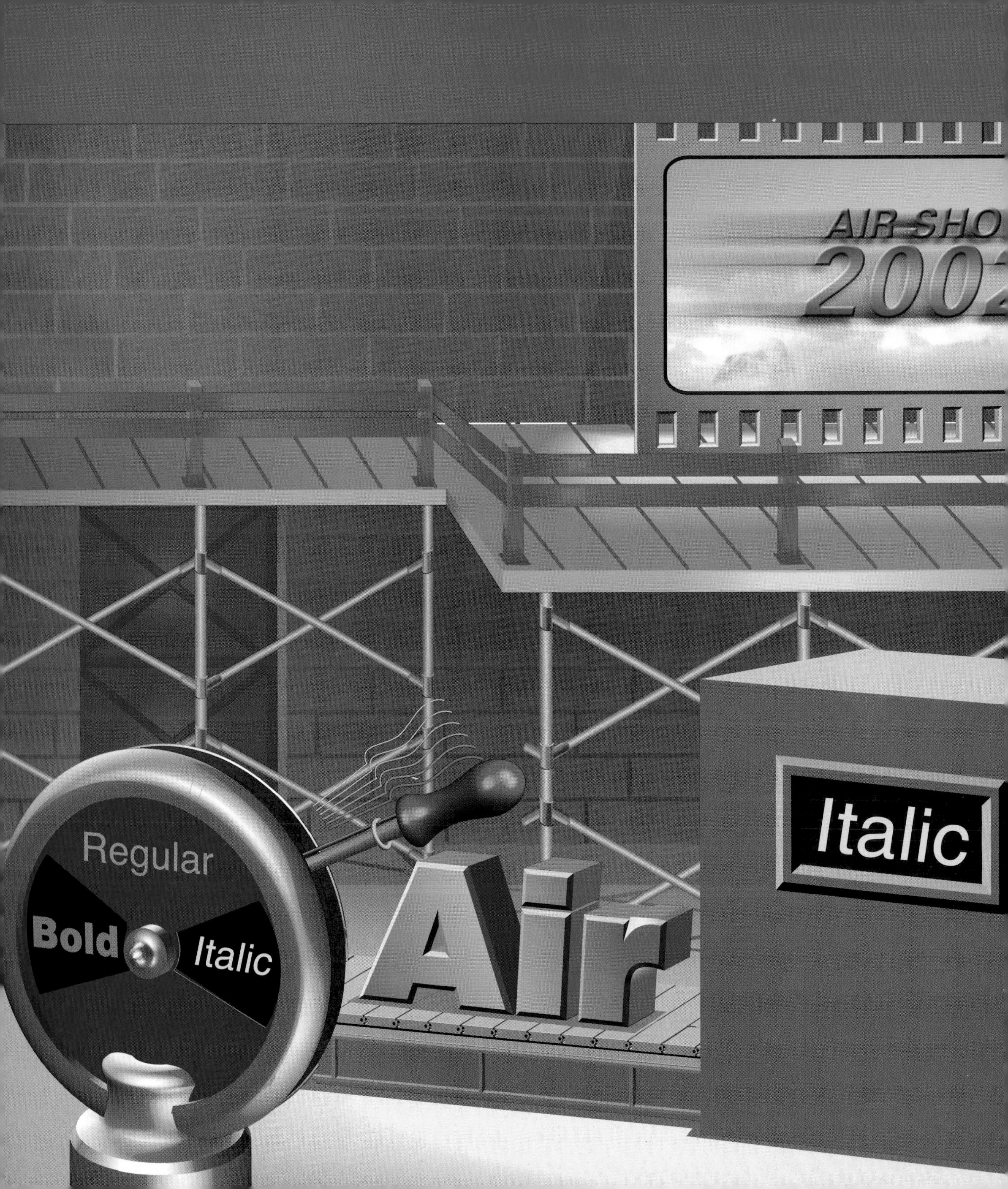
AIR SHO
2002
Regular
Bold
Italic
Air
Italic

CHAPTER 12

Creating Text and Graphic Effects

Does your video need a title? Do you want to add a geometric shape or design your own logo? This chapter shows you how to add title clips and shapes to your project.

UNDERSTANDING TEXT AND GRAPHIC ELEMENTS

You can use text and graphic elements in your video to convey information, create a mood, introduce a scene, and more. This section gives you an overview of the kinds of text and graphic elements you can create.

Title Clips

Adding titles to a project can make your video more professional, help viewers identify key parts, and introduce important information such as names and dates. Although essentially static, *title clips* can be used on their own for any number of frames in your project, or you can superimpose them over other clips.

Why Add Graphics?

You can add simple graphic objects, such as shapes or lines, to a title clip to dress it up. You can also use graphic objects on their own, without text, if needed. For example, you may create a logo or graphic symbol to use at key moments in the video.

Text and Drawing Tools

Titles and graphic objects are created in Premiere's Title window. The Title window includes simple drawing tools you can use to create shapes and line objects. The window also includes tools for entering and formatting text to use in your video. You can combine the text and drawing tools to make eye-catching titles. For more advanced graphic objects, use a fully-loaded graphics program such as Adobe Photoshop and import the graphic file into Premiere.

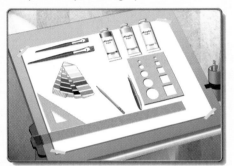

Scrolling Title Text

The Title window also offers a feature called the *Rolling Title tool* for creating text that scrolls or crawls across the screen. You may want to use scrolling text for your video's credits, or for the opening title sequence. The Rolling Title tool enables you to control the speed of the scroll as well as the direction in which the text moves.

Saving Title Clips

After you create your title text or graphic objects, you must save your work before you use them in the video. Title clip files are saved with the .ptl extension in Premiere. As soon as you save a title clip, it appears in the current video's Project window. You can also reuse the clip in other Premiere projects.

Applying Title Clips

When you are ready to use a title clip in your video, you simply add it to a track in the Timeline window. You can control exactly how long the clip plays, and whether it is superimposed over another clip or used on its own.

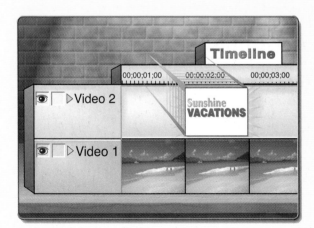

CREATE A NEW TITLE

You can add titles to your project using Premiere's titling feature. Titles are saved as static clips you can add to the project Timeline. You can also assign video effects to your titles as well as superimpose the title clips over other clips in your video.

See Chapters 14 and 15 to learn about superimposing and video effects.

CREATE A NEW TITLE

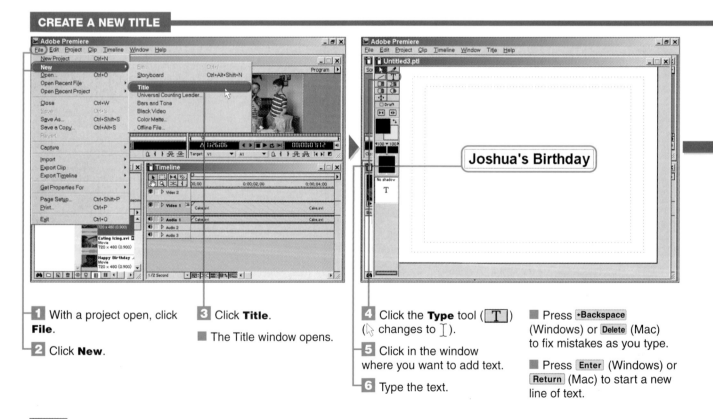

1 With a project open, click **File**.

2 Click **New**.

3 Click **Title**.

■ The Title window opens.

4 Click the **Type** tool (T) (changes to I).

5 Click in the window where you want to add text.

6 Type the text.

■ Press +Backspace (Windows) or Delete (Mac) to fix mistakes as you type.

■ Press Enter (Windows) or Return (Mac) to start a new line of text.

Can I control the size of the Title window?

Yes. With the Title window open,
click **Window**, **Window
Options**, and then **Title
Window Options** to open the
Title Window Options dialog box.
From here you can set a window
size, a background color, an
aspect ration (screen width to
screen height), title size for
television screen, and
NTSC-safe colors to
ensure color compatibility
with video monitors. Make
your selections and click
OK. You can also click and
drag any window edge to
resize the window.

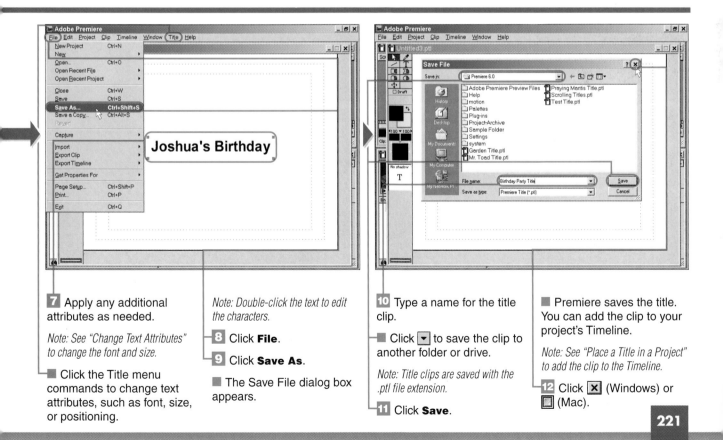

7 Apply any additional
attributes as needed.

*Note: See "Change Text Attributes"
to change the font and size.*

■ Click the Title menu
commands to change text
attributes, such as font, size,
or positioning.

*Note: Double-click the text to edit
the characters.*

8 Click **File**.

9 Click **Save As**.

■ The Save File dialog box
appears.

10 Type a name for the title
clip.

■ Click ▼ to save the clip to
another folder or drive.

*Note: Title clips are saved with the
.ptl file extension.*

11 Click **Save**.

■ Premiere saves the title.
You can add the clip to your
project's Timeline.

*Note: See "Place a Title in a Project"
to add the clip to the Timeline.*

12 Click ☒ (Windows) or
▢ (Mac).

CHANGE TEXT ATTRIBUTES

You can change the appearance of title text, including the font and size, or control the positioning of text, called *justification* or *alignment*. The Title menu contains commands commonly found among word-processing programs for changing text attributes.

CHANGE TEXT ATTRIBUTES

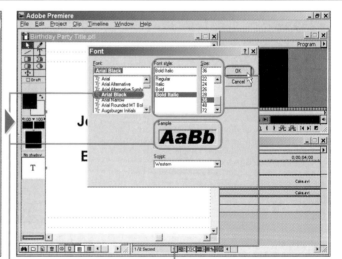

CHANGE THE FONT

1 With the Title window open, double-click over the title text.

Note: See the section "Create a New Title" to open the Title window.

2 Click and drag over the text you want to change.

■ The text is selected.

3 Click **Title**.

4 Click **Font**.

■ The Font dialog box appears.

5 Click a font.

■ Click the scroll arrows to view the complete list of available fonts.

■ This area displays a sample of the selected font.

■ You can also click to select a font style and size.

6 Click **OK**.

■ Premiere applies the new font.

Note: See the section "Create a New Title" to save a title clip.

How do I resize the text object in the Title window?

Every item you add to the Title window, either text or graphics, is an object that can be moved or resized in the window. Click the text on the Title window to reveal selection handles around the text object. Click and drag a selection handle (⍄ becomes 🖑) to resize the text object. To move the text object, click and drag the middle area of the text. To edit the text, double-click over the text and make your changes.

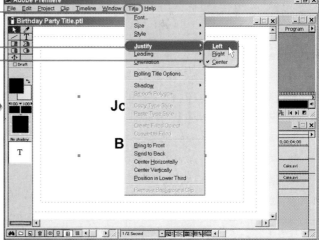

CHANGE TEXT ALIGNMENT

1 With the Title window open, click the **Selection** tool (🔲).

2 Click the text.

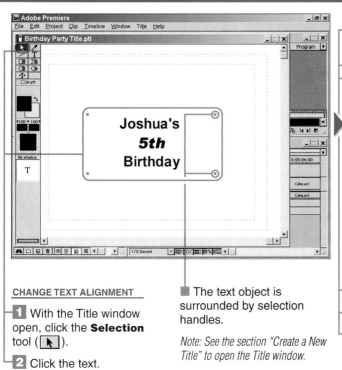

■ The text object is surrounded by selection handles.

Note: See the section "Create a New Title" to open the Title window.

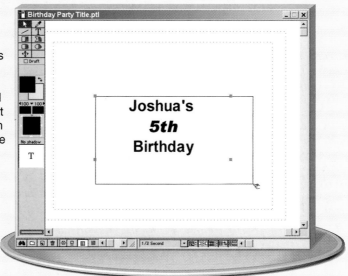

3 Click **Title**.

4 Click **Justify**.

5 Click an alignment setting.

■ Premiere immediately aligns the text.

Note: See the section "Create a New Title" to save a title clip.

APPLY A BACKGROUND FRAME

You can add a frame from a video clip to the background of your title to help you determine what font to use or assist you in the placement of graphic elements. The background frame is not saved as part of the title, but helps you determine attributes and placement for when you superimpose the title over a clip.

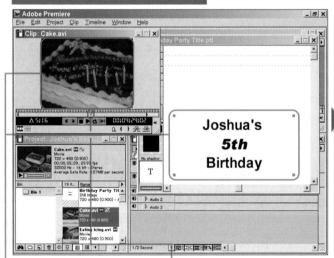

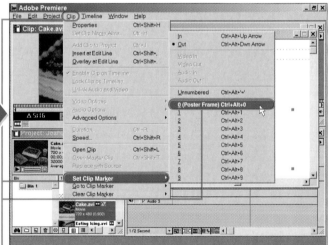

1 Display the Title window you want to edit.

Note: See the section "Create a New Title" to open the Title window.

2 Open the clip you want to use as the background.

Note: See Chapter 5 to work with clips.

3 Drag the Set Location marker (▽) to cue the clip to the frame you want to use.

4 Click **Clip**.

5 Click **Set Clip Marker**.

6 Click **0**.

■ Premiere sets the current frame as the background frame for the Title window.

7 Click ⊠ (Windows) or ▣ (Mac) to close the Clip window.

Can I use a color as a background instead of a frame from a clip?

Yes. With the Title window open, click **Window**, **Window Options**, and then **Title Window Options** to open the Title Window Options dialog box. Click **Background** to open the Color Picker dialog box, which contains a palette of colors from which you can choose. Click a color and click **OK**. To set an opaque background, click the **Opaque** check box. Click **OK** again to apply the color to the title clip.

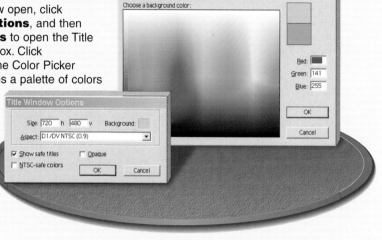

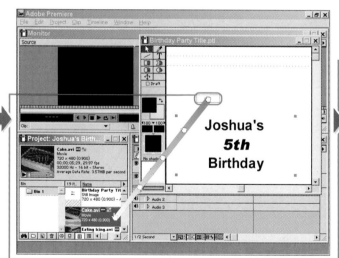

■8 Click and drag the clip to the Title window (👆 becomes 🖐).

Note: You may need to resize the Title window to see the Project window. Click and drag a window edge to resize the window.

■ The frame appears as the background behind the title text.

*Note: To remove the frame, click **Title** and then **Remove Background Clip**.*

■ You can now create or edit the title text to work with the frame background.

Note: See the section "Create a New Title" to create and save a title clip.

CREATE A SCROLLING TITLE

You can create a scrolling title that makes text scroll or crawl across the screen. Scrolling titles are good for long sequences of text, such as credits at the end of a project. Using the Rolling Title tool, you can control how fast the text scrolls as well as which direction it moves. The speed of the scrolling motion is determined by the length of the clip.

CREATE A SCROLLING TITLE

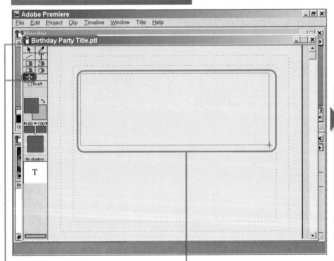

1 Display the Title window.

Note: See the section "Create a New Title" to open the Title window.

2 Click the **Rolling Title** tool (▨) (▯ changes to +).

3 Click and drag an area within the Title window where you want the scrolling text to appear.

■ A scrollable text box appears.

4 Type the text you want to use as scrolling text.

■ You can click and drag a selection handle to resize the scrolling text area.

5 Click **Title**.

6 Click **Rolling Title Options**.

■ The Rolling Title Options dialog box appears.

I created scrolling text, but it does not seem to scroll anywhere. Why not?

You may need to readjust the size of the text object area to achieve a scrolling result. Try making the text object smaller in size. For example, shorten the depth of the text area so it only takes up half the screen. Also experiment with making the text scroll in another direction to see if the scroll effect is more noticeable.

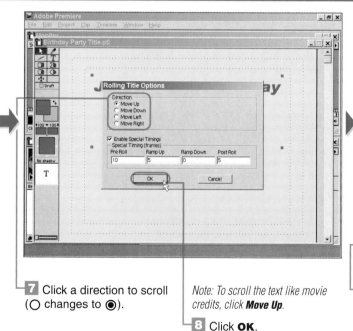

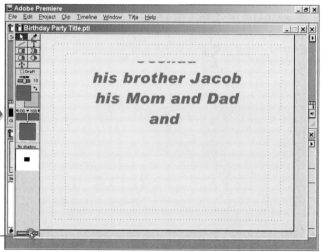

7 Click a direction to scroll (○ changes to ◉).

*Note: To scroll the text like movie credits, click **Move Up**.*

8 Click **OK**.

9 Click and drag the scrolling slider to see the scrolling text effect.

Note: See the section "Create a New Title" to save a title clip.

CREATE A GRAPHIC SHAPE

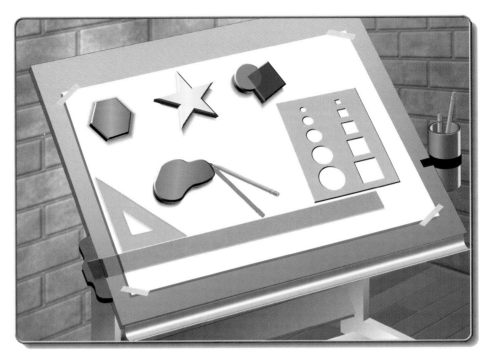

Using the Title window's simple drawing tools, you can create simple illustrations to enhance your title text. For example, you can combine circles, ovals, squares, and rectangles, and add fill colors. You can also draw lines and freeform shapes.

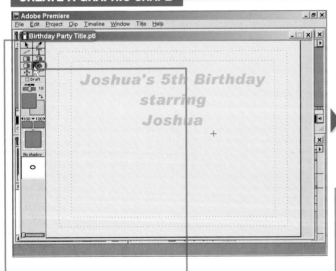

DRAW AN OUTLINE SHAPE

1 Open the Title window.

Note: See the section "Create a New Title" to open the Title window.

2 Click the left side of any shape tool (⌖ changes to +).

■ In this example, the **Oval** tool ( ) is selected.

3 Click and drag a shape in the Title window area.

Note: See the section "Format Graphic Shapes" to change shape attributes.

How do I draw a line?

Click the **Line** tool , and then click and drag the line shape in the Title window. You can click and drag the **Line Width** slider to set a different thickness for the line or click the **Object Color** box to set another color for the line. To resize a line object, just click and drag an end point on the selected line.

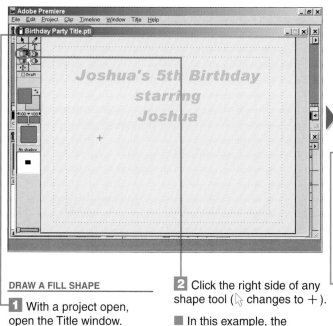

DRAW A FILL SHAPE

1 With a project open, open the Title window.

Note: See the section "Create a New Title" to open the Title window.

2 Click the right side of any shape tool (⬚ changes to +).

■ In this example, the **Rectangle** tool (⬚) is selected.

3 Click and drag a shape in the Title window area.

Note: See the section "Format Graphic Shapes" to change the fill color.

FORMAT GRAPHIC SHAPES

You can change the attributes of any graphic shape that you add to a title clip. For example, you may want to change a shape's fill color, or change the thickness of a line.

FORMAT GRAPHIC SHAPES

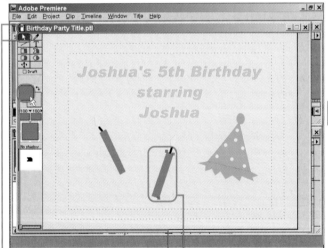

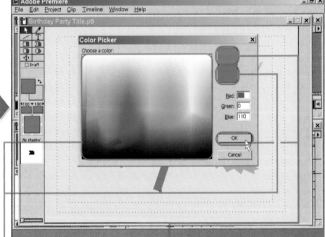

CHANGE THE OBJECT COLOR

■1 Display the Title window.

Note: See "Create a New Title" to open the Title window.

■2 Click the **Selection** tool (▶).

■3 Click the object you want to edit.

■4 Click the **Object Color** box.

■ The Color Picker dialog box appears.

■5 Click a color from the palette.

■ A sample of the color appears here.

■ The current color appears here.

■6 Click **OK**.

■ Premiere applies the new color choice.

230

How do I create a gradient effect?

You can create *gradient effects,* which are blends of color intensity, for Object Color or Shadow Color. Click the right or left gradient color box and choose a color from the Color Picker dialog box. To change gradient intensity, click the arrow next to the left or right gradient box and drag the slider to a new setting.

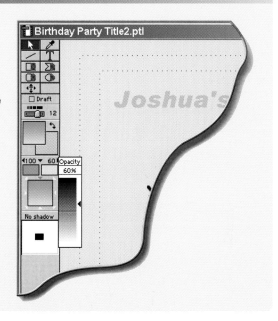

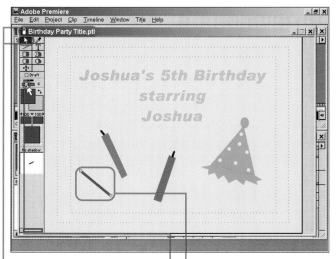

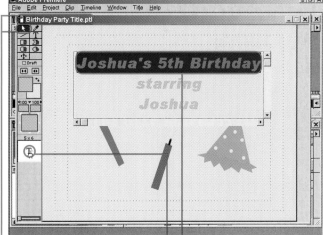

CHANGE THE LINE THICKNESS

1 Display the Title window.

Note: See "Create a New Title" to open the Title window.

2 Click the **Selection** tool (▶).

3 Click the line object you want to edit.

4 Click and drag the **Line Width** slider (▣).

■ The selected object's line thickness changes.

ADD A DROP SHADOW

1 Display the Title window.

Note: See "Create a New Title" to open the Title window.

2 Click the **Selection** tool (▶).

3 Click the object or select the text you want to edit.

4 Click and drag the **Shadow Positioner** (T) to create the drop shadow.

■ Premiere adds a drop shadow to the object.

231

EDIT A TITLE CLIP

You can reopen any title clip you create and make edits to the text or graphics. For example, you may need to edit the spelling, or change the color of a shape.

EDIT A TITLE CLIP

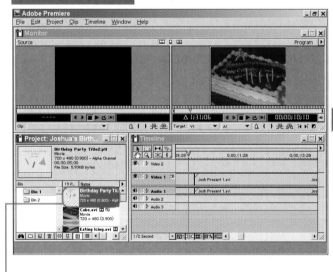

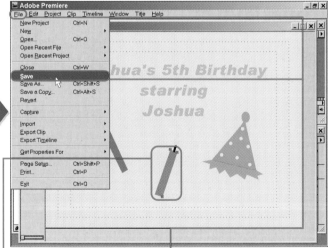

1 Double-click the title clip.

Note: See the section "Create a New Title" to create and save a title.

■ Premiere opens the title in the Title window.

2 Edit the title text or graphic elements as needed.

Note: See the previous sections to add text and graphic objects.

3 Click **File**.

4 Click **Save**.

■ The title changes are saved.

PLACE A TITLE IN A PROJECT

After you create a title clip, you can place it in your project. When you save a title clip, it is added to the Project window of the current project. You can quickly insert it into a track on the project Timeline.

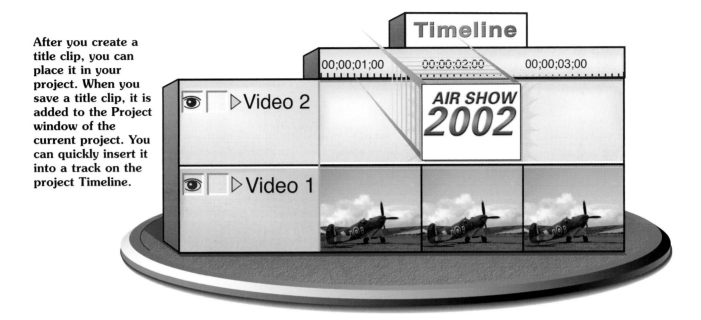

PLACE A TITLE IN A PROJECT

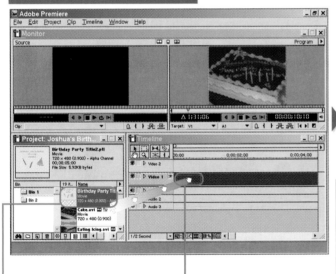

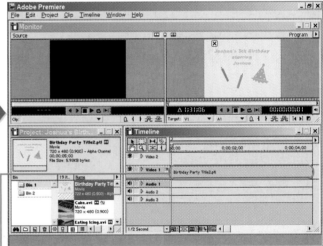

1 Click the title clip in the Project window.

Note: See the section "Create a New Title" to create and save a title.

2 Click and drag the title clip to the Timeline (changes to).

■ The title is added to the project.

Note: See Chapter 14 to superimpose clips. See Chapter 6 to work with tracks on the Timeline.

CHAPTER 13

Creating Video Effects

Are you ready to spice up your video project with special effects? In this chapter, you learn how to apply all kinds of image effects and control them using keyframes.

Keyframe

Keyframe

UNDERSTANDING VIDEO EFFECTS

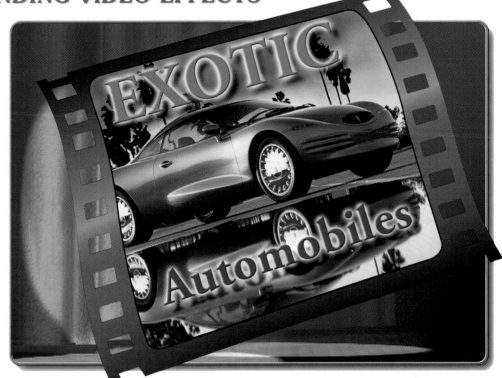

You can use video effects to add visual interest to your project. For example, you can assign a video effect to a clip that makes the clip appear to blur or shake. Or you may want to add an effect that makes a title clip seem to glow. Before you get started, take a look at the basic concepts behind video effects.

What Exactly Is a Video Effect?

A *video effect* is a filter that enhances or alters the video image. You can apply video effects to any clip in your project. Premiere includes 74 video effects that you can apply. You can assign multiple effects to the same clip. Premiere plays the effects in the order in which they are added. You can also reorder the effects as needed.

What Types of Effects Are Available?

Premiere's Video Effects palette includes 14 folders, each listing one or more effects. Premiere includes effects that change the image brightness and contrast, blur and distort the image, and create waves and swirls in the image.

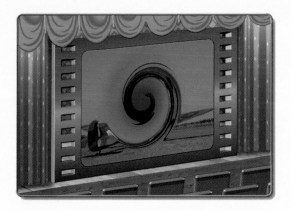

Fine-Tuning Effects

In addition to assigning an effect, you can also adjust its properties to customize it to meet your particular needs. Each effect offers different options. For example, the Alpha Glow effect, located in the Stylize folder, provides sliders for you to move to adjust the glow intensity and brightness as well as a color option for changing the color of the effect.

Understanding Keyframes

Every video effect includes at least two keyframes — a start keyframe and an end keyframe. A *keyframe* marks a key change in the content or attributes. You may add a keyframe to the middle of the clip and adjust the effect properties to create a change in the effect. For example, the effect may start with one color, switch to another color at a keyframe in the middle of the clip, and then finish in a third color.

Editing Keyframes

You can add, delete, and move keyframes on the timeline. The closer the keyframes, the faster the effect. You cannot, however, remove the start and end keyframes. You can, however, move them to start or end the effect at a different point in the clip, but every effect must include a start and end keyframe.

Calculating In-Between Frames

Every time you add a keyframe and make a change in the effect, Premiere calculates the changes between keyframes for you. As long as you define two keyframes, Premiere interpolates all the frames in-between to get from the first keyframe to the next. When you add a keyframe, Premiere duplicates the effect settings found in the previous keyframe. You can then make changes to the effect properties to change the effect.

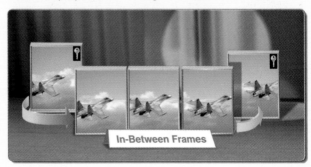

APPLY A VIDEO EFFECT

Crystallize Effect

You can apply video effects to your project for added visual interest. Video effects, also called *filters*, are used to alter or enhance the video image. You can add as many effects as you like to a clip. Premiere includes 74 different video effects, found in the Video Effects palette.

See Chapter 1 to learn more about using Premiere palettes.

APPLY A VIDEO EFFECT

1 Click the clip to which you want to assign an effect.

2 Click **Window**.

3 Click **Show Video Effects**.

■ The Video Effects palette opens.

4 Click the effect you want to use.

■ Clicking ▷ opens a folder and lists associated effects.

■ Clicking ▽ closes a folder list.

■ Clicking ☒ (Windows) or ▣ (Mac) closes the palette entirely.

■ Click the scroll bar to view all the available folders and effects.

What are the icons that appear in front of the effect names?

The 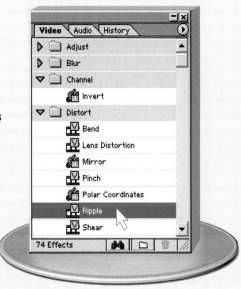 icons denote effects original to Premiere. The icons denote effects borrowed from Adobe's After Effects plug-in program, a program for designing visual effects. Effects with the icons can be viewed in both Premiere and After Effects.

5 Drag the effect from the palette and drop it onto the clip (☝ changes to ☝).

■ The effect is added to the clip, and the Effect Controls palette appears, enabling you to fine-tune the effect, if needed.

Note: Premiere adds each effect you assign to the Effect Controls palette list.

6 Click **Timeline**.

7 Click **Preview**.

Note: You can also press **Enter** *(Windows) or* **Return** *(Mac) to begin the preview process.*

■ Premiere builds a preview, which plays in the Monitor window showing any video effects assigned.

Note: See "Adjust Effect Settings" to fine-tune the effect.

ADJUST EFFECT SETTINGS

Depending on the video effect you are using, you can use additional controls to fine-tune the performance of the effect. Property values for an effect are found in the Effect Controls palette. The palette lists all the effects assigned to a clip. The number and type of values you can adjust vary from controlling color and opacity to positioning.

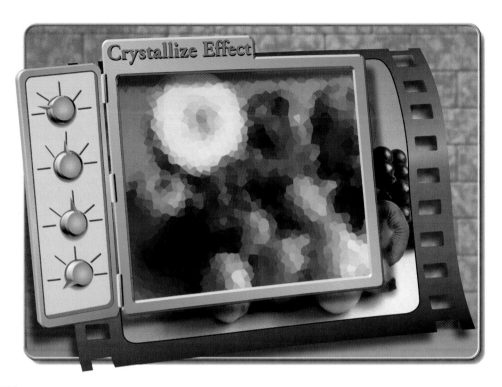

ADJUST EFFECT SETTINGS

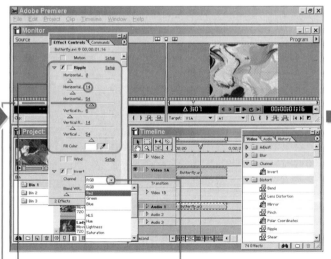

1 Click the clip containing the effect you want to adjust.

2 Click **Window**.

3 Click **Show Effect Controls**.

■ The Effect Controls palette opens.

4 Use any of the available controls to adjust the effect's property values.

■ Clicking and dragging ◢ decreases or increases the value.

■ Clicking ▾ displays a menu of options.

■ Clicking an underlined value displays an additional dialog box of options.

What happened to the video effects included with Premiere 5?

For backward compatibility, Premiere 6 offers several effects found in earlier versions. To find them, click the Video Effects menu button and click **Show Hidden**. This command displays the Obsolete folder in the palette, and you can choose from the effects you may be used to using from previous versions of Premiere.

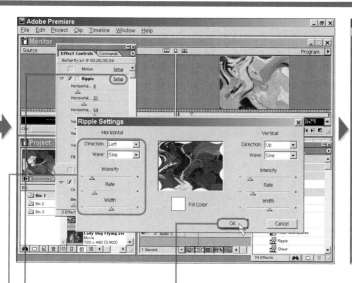

5 Click **Setup**.

■ The effect's Settings dialog box opens.

6 Make changes to the settings as needed.

■ The settings available vary based on the type of effect. This example shows the Ripple effect's settings.

7 Click **OK**.

■ To preview the adjustments, press `Enter` (Windows) or `Return` (Mac).

■ The preview plays in the Monitor window, showing any video effects assigned.

■ Clicking here closes the Effect Controls palette.

REMOVE AND DISABLE EFFECTS

You can either remove an effect that you no longer need and have Premiere delete it from the clip, or you can disable the effect but keep it listed in the Effect Controls palette. Disabling an effect retains its settings but excludes the effect from any previewing or exporting actions.

REMOVE EFFECTS

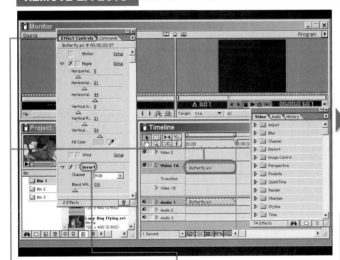

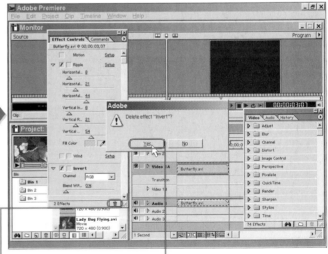

1 Click the clip containing the effect you want to remove.

2 Display the Effect Controls palette.

Note: See the section "Adjust Effect Settings" to open the Effect Controls palette.

3 Click the name of the effect you want to remove.

4 Click the **Delete** (🗑) button.

■ Premiere displays a warning box.

5 Click **Yes** to remove the effect.

Can I change the order in which effects are listed in the Effect Controls palette?

Yes. Premiere plays the effects in the order listed in the Effect Controls palette. To change the order, click an effect name and then drag the effect up or down in the list.

DISABLE EFFECTS

-1 Click the clip containing the effect you want to remove.

-2 Display the Effect Controls palette.

Note: See the section "Adjust Effect Settings" to open the Effect Controls palette.

-3 Click the **Enable Effect** box.

■ The 🗲 icon disappears and the effect is disabled.

*Note: Click the **Enable Effect** box again to toggle the effect back on.*

CHANGE A VIDEO EFFECT USING KEYFRAMES

You can use keyframes to change effect properties at key points in the Timeline. For example, you may want to change the Alpha Glow effect color in the middle of the clip. All effects include a start and end keyframe. You can add additional keyframes between them to mark key changes in the effect. Premiere calculates the values between two keyframes to achieve the desired change.

CHANGE A VIDEO EFFECT USING KEYFRAMES

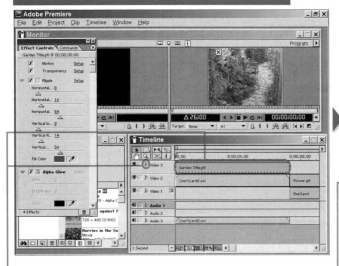

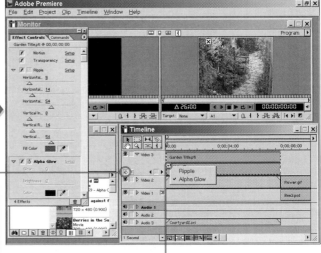

1 Click the clip containing the effect you want to adjust.

2 Click ▷.

Note: See Chapter 7 to learn more about working with tracks in the Timeline window.

3 If the clip is on Video Track 2 or higher, click ◇ to display the keyframe line.

■ If the clip has more than one effect assigned, click here and click the effect you want to adjust.

Can I delete a start or end keyframe?

No, you cannot remove the default start and end keyframes of an effect, but you can move them. Moving the start or end keyframe changes where the effect is applied in the Timeline.

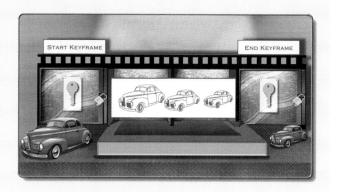

4 Click and drag the 🖳 to where you want to change the effect.

5 Click ☑.

■ Premiere adds a keyframe to the timeline.

6 In the Effect Controls palette, change the desired property values.

Note: See the section "Adjust Effect Settings" to open the Effect Controls palette.

■ You can continue adding keyframes as needed.

7 Press **Enter** (Windows) or **Return** (Mac) to preview the effect.

■ Premiere builds a preview and the video plays in the Monitor window.

EDIT VIDEO EFFECT KEYFRAMES

You can edit keyframes on the Timeline to change the speed of, or make additional changes to the effect. For example, you can move two keyframes closer together to speed up the effect, or you may need to remove a keyframe.

EDIT VIDEO EFFECT KEYFRAMES

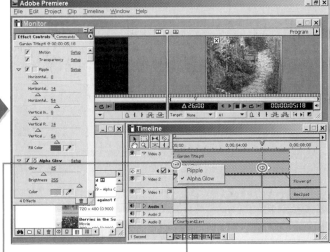

MOVE A KEYFRAME

■1 Click the clip containing the effect you want to adjust.

■2 Click ▽ .

Note: See Chapter 7 to learn more about working with tracks.

■3 If the clip is on Video Track 2 or higher, click ◇ to display the keyframe line.

■ If the clip has more than one effect assigned, you can click here and then click the effect you want to adjust.

■4 Click and drag the keyframe to a new position.

How do I remove all the keyframes I added?

To remove all keyframes except the start and end keyframe, which all effects must include, click ⏱ for the effect in the Effect Controls palette. Premiere displays a warning box; click **Yes** to delete all extra keyframes.

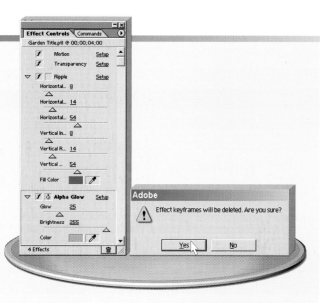

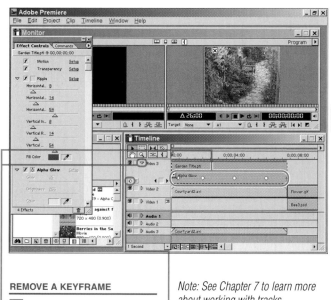

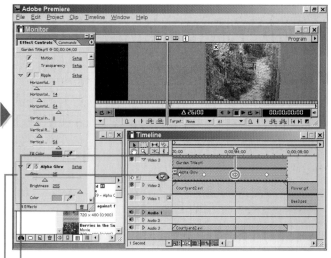

REMOVE A KEYFRAME

1 With a project open, click the clip containing the effect you want to adjust.

2 Click ▷.

Note: See Chapter 7 to learn more about working with tracks.

3 If the clip is on Video Track 2 or higher, click ◇ to display the keyframe line.

4 Click the keyframe you want to remove.

5 Click ✓.

■ Premiere removes the keyframe from the Timeline.

Note: See the section "Change a Video Effect Using Keyframes" to add keyframes to the Timeline.

Similarity = 0

Blend = 0

Threshold = 0

Cutoff = 0

CHAPTER 14

Superimposing Clips

Do you want to learn how to superimpose clips? This chapter tells you what you need to know to make clips transparent in your video.

UNDERSTANDING TRANSPARENCY IN PREMIERE

You can superimpose one clip over another by making the top clip transparent. By setting a clip's opacity, you can make video images fade in and out in your project. If you are new to setting transparency controls in Premiere, this section gives you some important background information.

What Is Superimposing?

When you superimpose a clip, you make the clip transparent to some degree. For example, you may superimpose a title clip over a video clip and make the title clip fade away after a few frames. By setting an opacity level, or *fade,* you tell Premiere how much of a transparency effect to create. You can use Premiere's *alpha channel,* an image layer that can be treated as different levels of transparency, to define transparency for titles or graphics.

Opacity Levels

If you set a clip to 100% opacity, the image is not transparent. If you set a clip to 0% opacity, the image becomes completely transparent. Any other opacity setting between 0 and 100 changes the transparency level intensity. For example, a clip set to 50% opacity is half transparent. You can control opacity by adjusting points on a track's Opacity Rubberband or fade line.

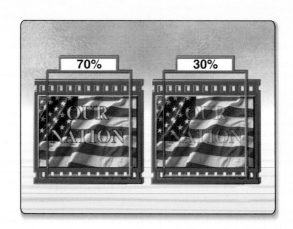

Track Hierarchy

Track hierarchy determines clip transparency. You can superimpose as many as 97 tracks, but you cannot superimpose Video Track 1. Only Video Track 2 and higher can be superimposed over other tracks. By layering clips in tracks, you can create transparent overlays to create fading and keying effects in your video.

Fading

The easiest way to superimpose two clips is to place one clip in a higher track over another clip in a lower track and adjust the higher clip's fade line. Fading involves changing the higher clip's opacity level.

Keying

Another way to superimpose clips is to make particular parts of one clip transparent using a *key*. *Keying* refers to making one image peek through to another, much like looking through a keyhole. The clip on the lowest track becomes the image in the keyhole while the clip on the highest track provides the shape for the keyhole.

Types of Keys

Premiere provides 15 types of keys for you to assign to a clip. You can either use a clip's alpha channel as a key or key out parts of an image based on color or luminance. Matte keys turn an image into the key shape. To learn about every type of key in Premiere, be sure to check out the program's help files. See Chapter 1 to learn how to access help, and Chapter 15 for information about alpha channels.

FADE A TRACK

You can *fade* a track over another track to superimpose the images. Fading a track changes the opacity of the clip. For example, you can fade a title clip over a video clip. You can fade in a clip to make it gradually visible or fade out to make it gradually disappear.

You can superimpose any track except Video Track 1.

1 Place one clip in one track and another clip directly above the first clip.

■ In this example a title clip in Video Track 2 is placed over a video clip in Video Track 1.

Note: See Chapter 7 to add and move clips.

2 Click the top clip.

3 Click ▷.

■ Premiere expands the track in the Timeline.

4 Click 🔲.

■ The red fade line, also called the Opacity Rubberband, is revealed.

Note: See Chapter 6 to learn more about using the Timeline window.

**How can I check the opacity
levels of a fade handle?**

Click a fade handle, click
Window, and then click
Show Info to display the
Info palette, where you can
quickly see the opacity
setting for that particular
point on the fade line. The
opacity level appears at the
bottom of the palette window.

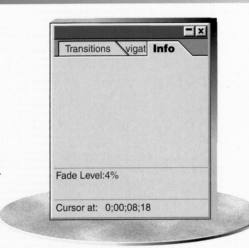

5 Click and drag the left or
right fade handle up or down
to increase or decrease the
fade opacity (changes
to).

■ The higher you drag the
handle, the more solid the
image. The lower you drag,
the more faded the image
becomes.

■ To gradually fade the top
clip, move the right end of
the fade line down at the end
of the clip.

6 Press **Enter** (Windows)
or **Return** (Mac).

■ Premiere previews the
effect in the Monitor window.

*Note: See Chapter 2 to save your
project file.*

FADE A TRACK USING FADE CONTROLS

You can control a fade effect's opacity at a given point in the Timeline with the Opacity Rubberband feature. By default, a superimposed clip includes two fade handles, one at the beginning and one at the end.

FADE A TRACK USING FADE CONTROLS

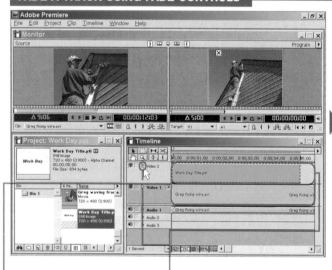

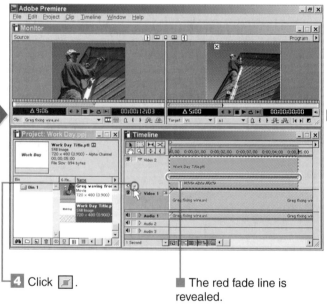

1 Place one clip in one track and another clip directly above the first clip.

■ In this example, a title clip in Video Track 2 is placed over a video clip in Video Track 1.

Note: See Chapter 7 to add and move clips.

2 Click the top clip.

3 Click ▷.

■ Premiere expands the track in the Timeline.

4 Click ■.

■ The red fade line is revealed.

Note: See Chapter 6 to learn more about using the Timeline window.

Can I use tools in the Timeline toolbox to edit the fade line?

Yes. You can use the Fade Scissors tool ✂ to cut the Opacity Rubberband and create two handles for you to move separately. You can then use the Fade Adjustment tool ↕ to move sections of the segmented fade line. See Chapter 7 to learn more about using the Timeline window's editing tools.

5 Click the fade line to create a fade handle (⌖ changes to ✤).

6 Click and drag the fade handle up or down to increase or decrease the fade opacity.

■ Dragging a handle upward makes the image more solid.

■ Dragging a handle downward makes the image more transparent.

Note: To remove a handle you no longer need, click and drag it off the track.

7 Continue adding more fade handles and placing them as needed.

8 Press `Enter` (Windows) or `Return` (Mac).

■ Premiere previews the effect in the Monitor window.

UNDERSTANDING KEYS

One way to superimpose clips is to use *keys*. A key acts much like a keyhole, enabling you to view a part or parts of the underlying clip. The key you assign designates the shape of the keyhole. Premiere offers 15 keys you can apply to create different types of transparency for a superimpose effect.

How Can I Use Keys?

You can utilize keys in numerous ways to create superimpose effects in your video. Remember that the overall effect of any key is to create a transparency effect for viewing the underlying clip or clips.

Luminance Keys

You can apply a *Luminance key* to define the transparent area of a superimposed clip by brightness levels. A Luminance key can key out the darkest pixels in the image leaving the brighter pixels opaque. Clips that show high contrasts in dark and light areas work best for Luminance keys. Premiere offers three types of Luminance keys: Luminance, Multiply, and Screen.

Chrominance Keys

Chrominance keys enable you to key out specific colors in the clip you are superimposing. Chrominance keys, called *Chroma keys* for short, are widely used to replace bluescreen or greenscreen backgrounds with another image. Chroma keys work best with subject matter, such as a person, filmed in front of a blue or green screen. Aside from the Chroma key, other chrominance keys include Blue Screen, Green Screen, RGB Difference, and Non-Red.

Alpha Channel Keys

You can apply an *Alpha Channel key* to key out an image that uses an alpha channel, such as images created in Adobe PhotoShop, After Effects, and Illustrator. An alpha key uses the clip's alpha channel to specify the transparent areas of the image. For example, most graphics are drawn on a white background. With an Alpha Channel key, you can make the white background transparent to see the underlying image that surrounds the graphic.

Matte Keys

Matte keys use a still or static image as the transparency for a superimposed clip. Matte keys include Image Matte, Track Matte, and Difference Matte. The Image Matte key, for example, makes black areas of the key transparent and white areas opaque.

Types of Key Parameters

Depending on the key you apply, a variety of parameters can be adjusted to fine-tune the effect. For example, if you apply a Luminance key, you can specify a threshold range for the darker pixel values and a cutoff range to set the opacity level. You adjust all key parameters with slider bars.

APPLY A KEY

You can use a key to make a specific part of an image transparent. When you apply a key to a clip superimposed over another clip, you determine what areas of the lower clip show through.

Premiere offers 15 different types of keys, including Luminance, Chrominance, Alpha Channel, and Matte keys.

APPLY A KEY

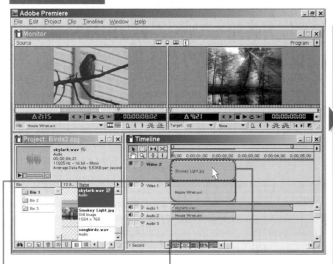

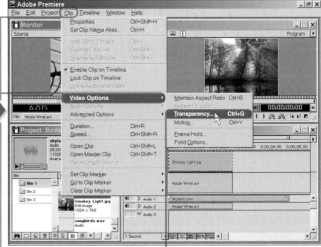

1 Place one clip directly above another clip in the Timeline window tracks.

■ In this example, a still image clip in Video Track 2 is placed over a video clip in Video Track 1.

Note: See Chapter 7 to add and move clips.

2 Click the top clip.

3 Click **Clip**.

4 Click **Video Options**.

5 Click **Transparency**.

■ The Transparency Settings dialog box appears.

I am using A/B edit mode and Premiere will not let me apply a key. Why not?

You cannot superimpose Video Track 1 in the Timeline window. If you are using A/B edit mode, the track is split into Video Track 1A and Video Track 1B. Both tracks still act as Video Track 1 and cannot be superimposed. Switch to Single-Track edit mode, or move the superimposed clips to higher tracks in the Timeline.

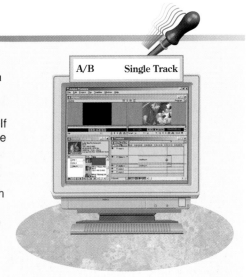

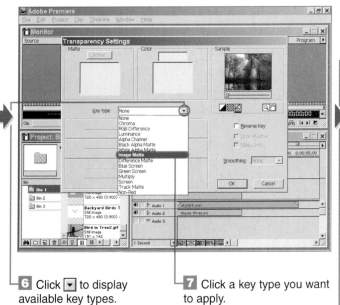

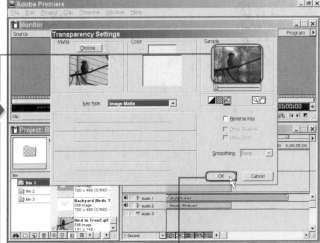

6 Click ▼ to display available key types.

7 Click a key type you want to apply.

■ Make any changes to the available key options, as needed.

■ You can preview the key here.

Note: See the section "Edit Key Settings" to learn more about previewing a key.

8 Click **OK**.

■ The key is applied.

■ Pressing **Enter** (Windows) or **Return** (Mac) previews the superimpose effect in the Monitor window.

EDIT KEY SETTINGS

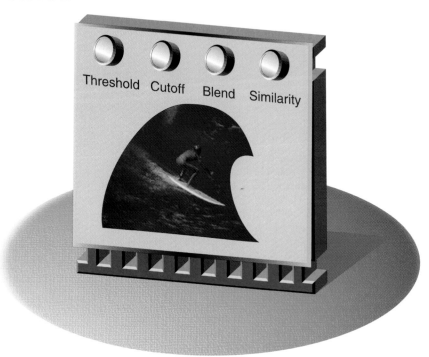

Threshold Cutoff Blend Similarity

You can edit a key to fine-tune the way in which the clip superimposes. For example, you can adjust the available parameters for a key and preview how the effect looks before applying it to a clip. The Transparency Settings dialog box offers several controls to help you analyze the key effect.

EDIT KEY SETTINGS

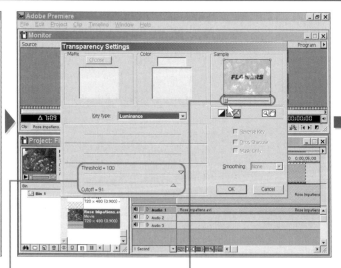

1 Click the clip containing the key you want to adjust.

Note: See "Apply a Key" to set a key.

2 Click **Clip**.

3 Click **Video Options**.

4 Click **Transparency**.

■ The Transparency Settings dialog box appears.

5 Make any changes to the available key parameters as needed.

■ Clicking and dragging adjusts a key parameter.

6 Clicking and dragging previews the effect.

What do the three check boxes below the Sample area do?

The three check box options are available only for particular keys. Click the **Reverse Key** option to invert the opaque and transparent areas of the effect. Click the **Drop Shadow** option to add a gray or opaque shadow to opaque areas of the effect. Click the **Mask Only** option to create a key that displays only the alpha channel matte of the clip.

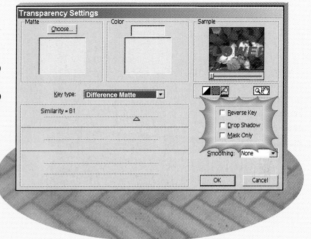

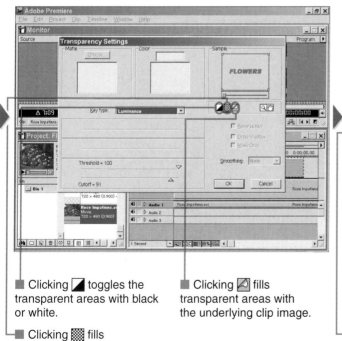

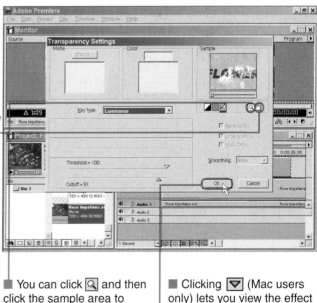

■ Clicking ◣ toggles the transparent areas with black or white.

■ Clicking ▨ fills transparent areas with the underlying clip image.

■ Clicking ▦ fills transparent areas with a checkerboard pattern.

■ You can click 🔍 and then click the sample area to zoom your view of the effect.

■ To view different areas of a zoomed sample, click ✋ and then click and drag the sample area.

■ Clicking ▽ (Mac users only) lets you view the effect in the Monitor window.

7 Click **OK**.

■ Any changes are applied to the superimpose effect.

APPLY A GARBAGE MATTE KEY

You can use a *garbage matte key* to key out areas of the clip frame you do not want to appear in the final key. For example, if your clip includes an unwanted object in the clip frame, referred to as "garbage" in video editing, you can mask it out so that it does not appear in the final superimpose effect.

APPLY A GARBAGE MATTE KEY

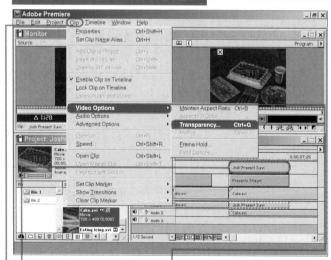

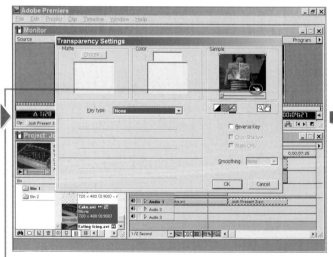

1 Click the clip to which you want to assign a key.

Note: See the section "Apply a Key" to prepare clips for a key effect.

2 Click **Clip**.

3 Click **Video Options**.

4 Click **Transparency**.

■ The Transparency Settings dialog box appears.

5 Click and drag the image handles in the Sample area to mask out the unwanted portion of the frame (becomes).

■ You can drag all four handles, or just one or two.

How do I smooth out the edges of a garbage matte?

If you use the garbage matte with the RGB Difference key, you can click the **Smoothing** ☑ and then click a smoothing option rather than assign a color. The Smoothing control sets anti-aliasing that blends the pixel colors to create a smoother edge.

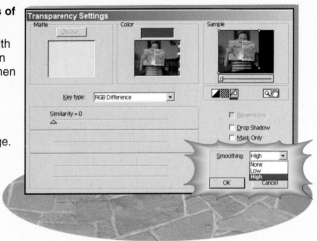

6 Click ☑.

7 Click a key name to apply that key.

Note: See the section "Understanding Keys" to learn more about key types.

■ If needed, make changes to the available key parameters.

8 Click **OK**.

■ Premiere applies the key to the clip.

■ Pressing Enter (Windows) or Return (Mac) previews the superimpose effect.

CREATE A SPLIT SCREEN EFFECT

You can use a key to create a split screen effect in your video. For example, with a presentation video, you may want to show a bulleted list of text on the left and a video clip on the right.

CREATE A SPLIT SCREEN EFFECT

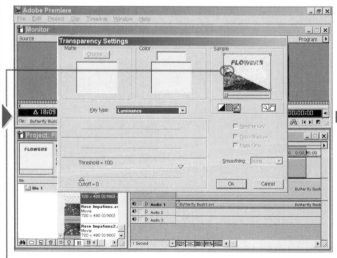

1 Click the clip to which you want to assign a split screen key.

Note: See the section "Apply a Key" to prepare clips for a key effect.

2 Click **Clip**.

3 Click **Video Options**.

4 Click **Transparency**.

■ The Transparency Settings dialog box appears.

5 Click and drag a top image handle in the Sample area to the area where you want the screen to split.

■  becomes ▧.

264

Can I split the screen in any direction and size?

Yes. You can split a screen horizontally, vertically, or even diagonally. The size of the split is determined by where you drag an image handle in the Sample area of the Transparency Settings dialog box.

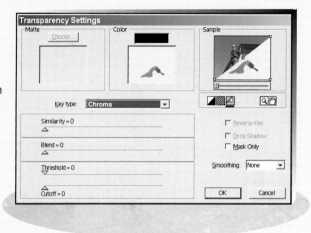

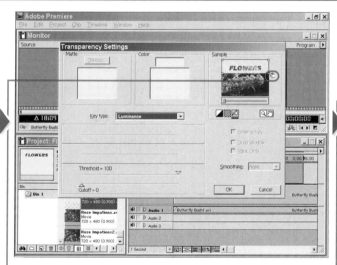

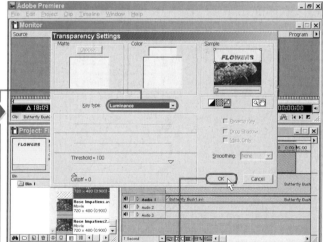

6 Click and drag a bottom image handle in the Sample area to match the same position as the top image handle.

7 Click ▾ .

8 Click the key you want to assign.

■ Make any changes to the available key parameters, as needed.

9 Click **OK**.

■ Premiere applies the key to the clip.

■ Pressing Enter (Windows) or Return (Mac) previews the superimpose effect.

...PREVIEWING...

PREVIEW
LOAD CLIP
MOVE KEYFRAME
CHANGE SPEED
REMOVE SETTING

CHAPTER 15

Creating Motion Effects

Are you ready to make your clips come alive? This chapter shows you how to animate your clips using Premiere's motion settings.

UNDERSTANDING MOTION EFFECTS

You can create dynamic animations in Premiere, called *motion effects,* which add movement to your video project. For example, you may want a still image to move from one side of the screen to the other, or you might want to make a video clip bounce across the frame. This section gives you some important background information about motion effects.

What Clips Can I Use?

You can create motion settings using a video clip, still image clip, or text clip. For example, you may want a company logo you have saved as a GIF file to appear to glide around the screen. If you use a video clip, you can make the entire clip move around the screen.

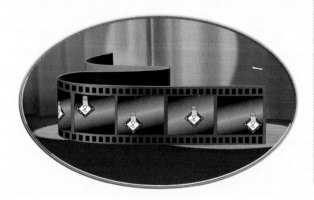

How Do Motion Effects Work?

A motion effect is comprised of a *path* with at least two keyframes. A path determines the movement of an effect. By default, the motion path moves from left to right, but you can set the path to move in any direction you want. Whatever path you specify, the clip follows, whether it is up and down, zigzag, or all over the frame. Motion settings apply to the entire clip.

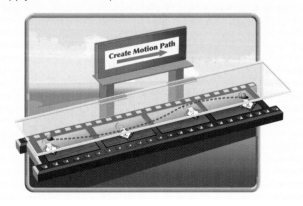

What are Keyframes?

A *keyframe* marks an important change in the motion path. For example, if a clip is following a zigzag path across the screen, you can use keyframes to mark a change in direction. In addition, keyframes can mark a change in the clip itself, such as size or rotation.

Types of Keyframe Changes

Premiere provides numerous effects settings that you can apply to your motion setting's keyframes. You can control the clip's Delay setting, for example, to make the clip seem to pause along the motion path. Or you can use the distortion settings to make the clip appear to distort as it travels along the path.

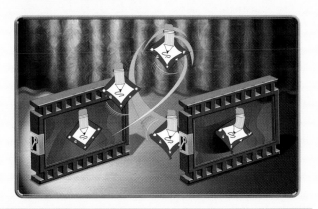

Save and Load Motion Settings

You can save a motion setting as a PMT file type and reuse the path again for another clip or in another project. To reuse the motion setting, you load the saved PMT file.

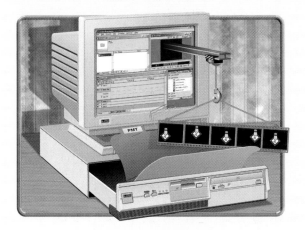

Using Alpha Channels

If you are using a still image that includes an *alpha channel,* you can mask out the image background and superimpose the clip over another video clip. An alpha channel is a grayscale image layer for creating transparency effects. This technique works only if you place the two clips in two different video tracks, one on top of the other.

ADD A MOTION SETTING TO A CLIP

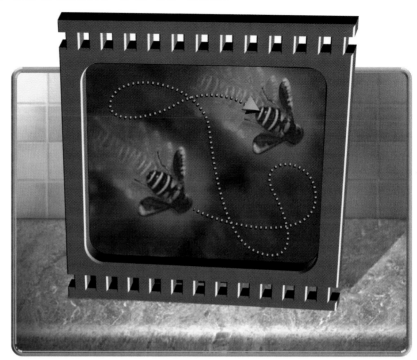

You can add a motion path to a clip to make the clip move around the frame. You can control the path of movement as well as rotate the clip and zoom in and out to make the clip larger or smaller. A motion path is based on keyframes that mark key changes along the path.

ADD A MOTION SETTING TO A CLIP

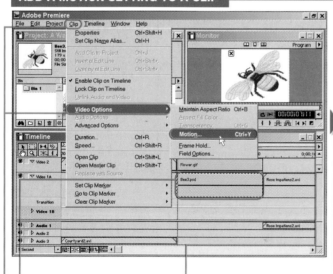

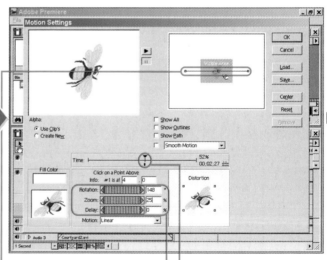

1 Click the clip to which you want to add a motion setting.

2 Click **Clip**.

3 Click **Video Options**.

4 Click **Motion**.

■ The Motion Settings dialog box appears.

Note: See the section "Understanding Motion Effects" to learn more about motion settings.

5 Add or adjust keyframes as needed to create your motion setting.

■ To add a keyframe, click the motion path (changes to).

■ You can also click the timeline to add a keyframe.

■ These controls let you change the clip's rotation, zoom, or delay.

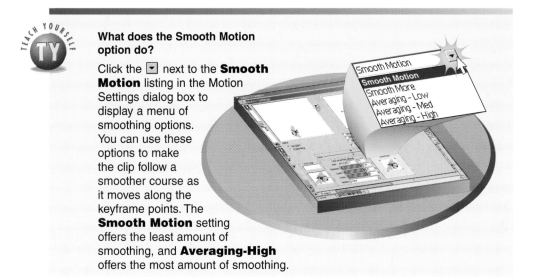

What does the Smooth Motion option do?

Click the ⏷ next to the **Smooth Motion** listing in the Motion Settings dialog box to display a menu of smoothing options. You can use these options to make the clip follow a smoother course as it moves along the keyframe points. The **Smooth Motion** setting offers the least amount of smoothing, and **Averaging-High** offers the most amount of smoothing.

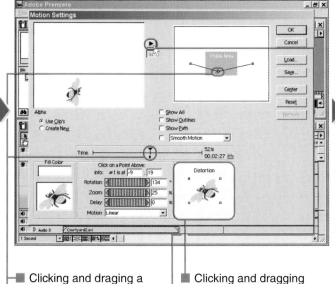

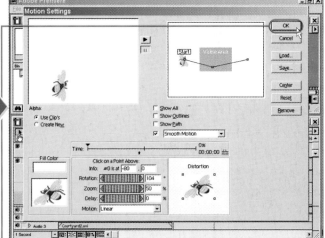

■ Clicking and draging a keyframe point changes the motion path.

■ You can also click and drag keyframe points on the Timeline to change the speed of the motion setting.

■ Clicking and dragging points creates distortion effects.

6 Click ▶ to preview the motion setting.

7 Click **OK**.

■ The clip adopts the motion settings.

Note: Clips with motion settings are marked with a red bar in the Timeline window.

■ Clicking **Save** saves the motion path as a motion settings file to reuse later.

■ Clicking **Load** loads a path you already saved.

■ Clicking **Reset** restores the default settings.

DEFINE A MOTION PATH

By adding and moving *keyframes* — key points of change along the path — you can tell Premiere exactly how you want a clip to move around the screen in a motion setting. By default, the motion path is set to move from left to right across the screen. By adding keyframes, you can make the path go in any direction, including off-screen.

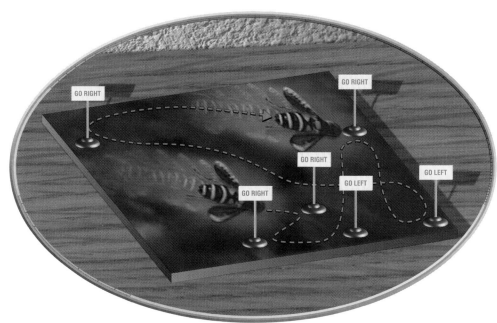

DEFINE A MOTION PATH

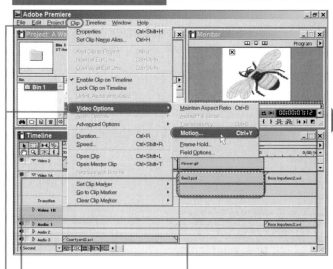

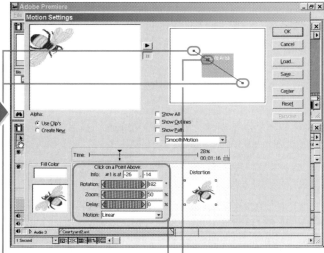

1 Click the clip to which you want to add a motion setting.

2 Click **Clip**.

3 Click **Video Options**.

4 Click **Motion**.

■ The Motion Settings dialog box appears.

Note: See the section "Understanding Motion Effects" to learn more.

5 Click and drag the start keyframe to the place you want to start the path.

6 Click and drag the end keyframe to the place you want to end the motion path.

7 Click the first point along the path in which you want to change direction.

■ Premiere inserts a new keyframe.

■ These controls let you change the clip's rotation, zoom, or delay to orient to the path change.

How can I make the motion setting pause at a keyframe?

Use the **Delay** attribute in the Motion Settings dialog box to pause the clip for a specific amount of time. The delay amount is a percentage of the clip's total time duration and based on keyframes. Simply put, you cannot set the delay to 2 seconds if the next keyframe is only 1 second away. You can also control motion speed by the placement of keyframes. See the section "Change Motion Speed" to learn more.

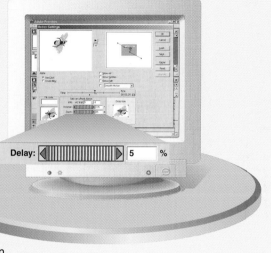

Delay: 5 %

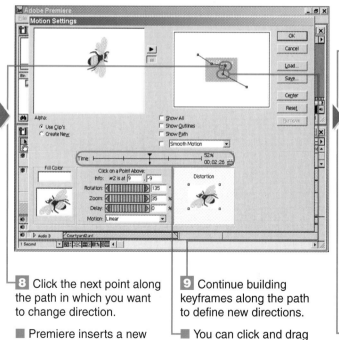

8 Click the next point along the path in which you want to change direction.

■ Premiere inserts a new keyframe.

9 Continue building keyframes along the path to define new directions.

■ You can click and drag keyframes on the Timeline to change the speed of the motion setting.

■ These options let you change how the path displays in the path area.

10 Click ▶ to preview the motion setting.

11 Click **OK**.

■ The clip adopts the motion setting.

273

CHANGE MOTION SPEED

When you create a motion path, the placement of keyframes along the path determines the animation's speed. You can make the effect appear to speed up or slow down at key points along the path without changing the path itself. Use the motion timeline in the Motion Settings dialog box to change keyframe distances.

CHANGE MOTION SPEED

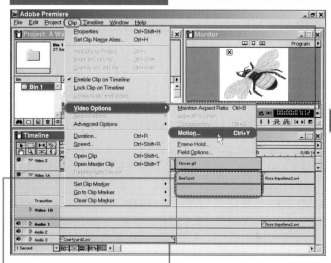

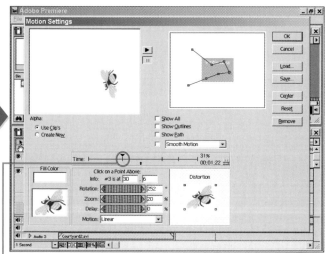

1 Click the clip containing the motion setting you want to adjust.

Note: See the section "Add a Motion Setting to a Clip" to add a motion setting.

2 Click **Clip**.

3 Click **Video Options**.

4 Click **Motion**.

■ The Motion Settings dialog box appears.

5 Click and drag the keyframe markers on the timeline.

Note: To add more keyframe markers to the Timeline, simply click the Timeline.

■ To increase the speed between two keyframes, click and drag one keyframe closer to the other.

How do I make my animation speed up at the end?

By default, Premiere plays the motion setting at a constant rate, called **Linear**, proceeding from one keyframe to the next. You can, however, make the animation appear to speed up or slow down using the Motion option in the Motion Settings dialog box. Click the **Motion** 🔽 and click **Accelerate** or **Decelerate**. The Accelerate setting makes the animation appear to play more quickly, and Decelerate makes the animation appear to slow down.

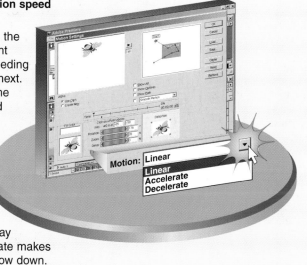

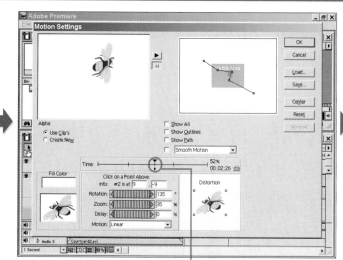

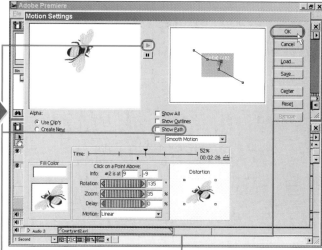

Note: To delete a keyframe marker, click the marker and press Delete.

■ To decrease the speed between two keyframes, click and drag one keyframe further away from the other.

Note: You can also drag a keyframe point on the motion path to move a keyframe.

6 Click ▶ to preview the changes.

■ Clicking here shows the speed between keyframes as dotted lines. The closer the dots appear, the faster the speed.

7 Click **OK**.

■ The motion setting is applied to the clip.

SET AN ALPHA CHANNEL

If you are superimposing a clip with motion settings over another video track, you can make the clip appear transparent so that the other clip is viewed as a background. For example, if you are assigning a motion setting to a title clip, you can use the title clip's alpha channel as a mask.

An *alpha channel* is an extra grayscale image layer Premiere uses to create transparency effects.

SET AN ALPHA CHANNEL

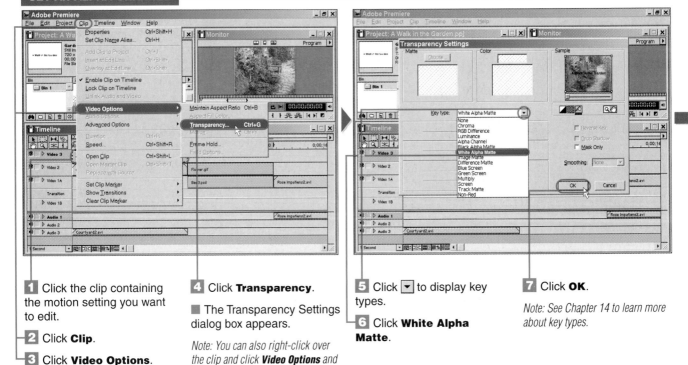

1 Click the clip containing the motion setting you want to edit.

2 Click **Clip**.

3 Click **Video Options**.

4 Click **Transparency**.

■ The Transparency Settings dialog box appears.

*Note: You can also right-click over the clip and click **Video Options** and then **Transparency**.*

5 Click ▼ to display key types.

6 Click **White Alpha Matte**.

7 Click **OK**.

Note: See Chapter 14 to learn more about key types.

276

Why does my motion effect seem to flash instead of move smoothly?

If the motion effect is too short, a strobe-light effect keeps you from seeing a motion blur. In this case, two or more keyframes are too close together. To remedy this, make sure that there is enough distance between keyframes to view the motion effect.

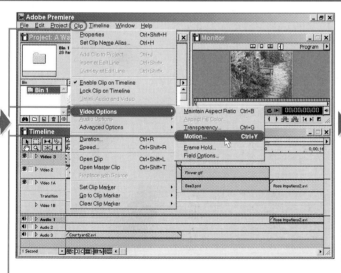

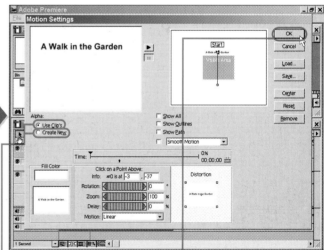

■8 Click **Clip**.

■9 Click **Video Options**.

■10 Click **Motion**.

■ The Motion Settings dialog box appears.

Note: See the section "Add a Motion Setting to a Clip" to learn more about motion settings.

■11 Click **Use Clip's** (○ changes to ◉).

■ To create a new alpha channel that matches the clip's frame, skip steps **2** through **7** and click here (○ changes to ◉).

■12 Click **OK**.

■ Premiere applies the clip's alpha channel to the motion setting.

SAVE A MOTION SETTING

You can save a motion setting to reuse again later, or to reuse in another project. When you save a motion setting, you save only the path and any assigned characteristics, such as zoom and rotation settings.

Premiere saves motion settings as files with a .pmt extension.

SAVE A MOTION SETTING

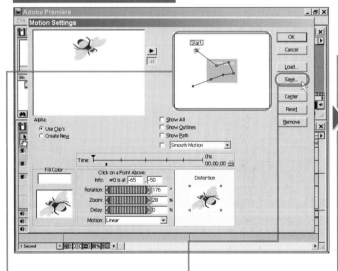

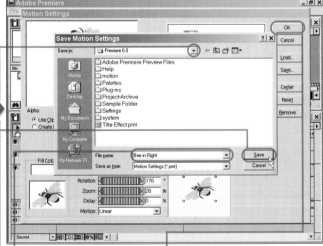

1 Create the motion setting using the Motion Setting dialog box.

Note: See the section "Add a Motion Setting to a Clip" to create a motion setting.

2 Click **Save**.

■ The Save Motion Settings dialog box appears.

3 Type a name for the file.

■ You can click ▾ to save the file to another folder or drive.

4 Click **Save**.

■ The motion setting is saved.

Note: See the section "Load a Motion Setting" to reuse the file.

5 Click **OK** to exit the Motion Settings dialog box.

LOAD A MOTION SETTING

You can reuse motion settings you have saved. For example, you may want to reuse the motion path with another clip in your project, or reuse it in another project file.

LOAD A MOTION SETTING

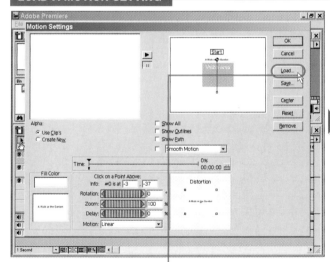

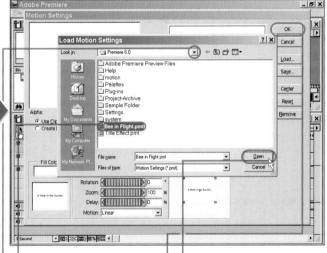

1 Click the clip in the Timeline window to which you want to assign the motion setting file.

2 Open the Motion Settings dialog box.

Note: See the section "Add a Motion Setting to a Clip" to open the Motion Settings dialog box.

3 Click **Load**.

■ The Load Motion Settings dialog box appears.

4 Click the motion setting file you want to assign.

■ You can click ▾ to locate the file in another folder or drive.

5 Click **Open**.

■ The motion setting is applied to the current clip.

6 Click **OK** to exit the Motion Settings dialog box.

279

PREVIEW A MOTION SETTING

After you assign a
motion setting, you can
preview how the setting
looks during playback.
When previewing a
motion setting, Premiere
must build the preview
file for playback in the
Monitor window.
Depending on the size of
the clip, processing
takes a few seconds to
several minutes to
complete.

PREVIEW A MOTION SETTING

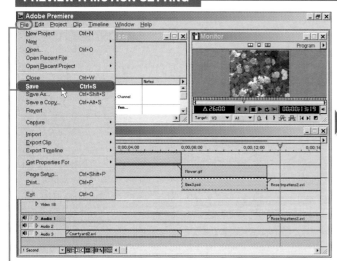

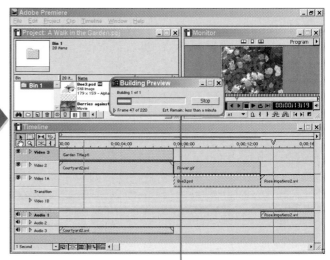

■1 Click **File**.

■2 Click **Save**.

*Note: See the Chapter 2 to learn
more about saving projects.*

■ Premiere saves the
changes you have made to
the project.

■3 Press **Enter** (Windows)
or **Return** (Mac).

*Note: You can also click **Timeline**,
then **Preview**.*

■ Premiere builds the
preview and plays the video
in the Monitor window.

*Note: To preview the motion setting
within the Motion Settings dialog
box, click ▶ .*

You can remove a
motion setting from
a clip and return the
clip to its original
state. Removing a
motion setting does
not affect a saved
motion setting file,
but simply
unattaches any
applied PMT file
from the clip.

REMOVE A MOTION SETTING

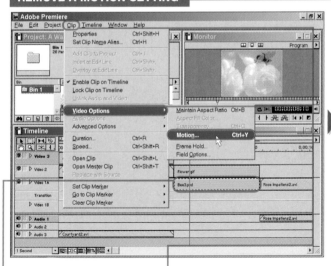

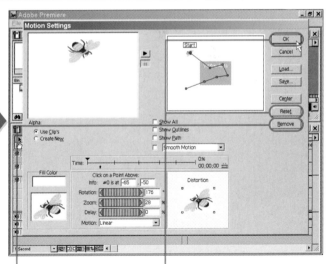

1 Click the clip containing
the motion setting you want
to remove.

*Note: See the section "Add a Motion
Setting to a Clip" to create a motion
setting.*

2 Click **Clip**.

3 Click **Video Options**.

4 Click **Motion**.

■ The Motion Settings dialog
box appears.

5 Click **Remove**.

■ The motion setting is
removed from the clip.

6 Click **OK** to close the
Motion Settings dialog box.

■ To restore the default
motion setting, click **Reset**.

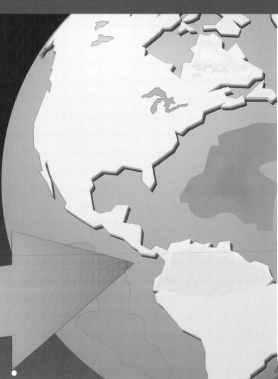

CHAPTER 16

Outputting Digital Video

Do you want to share your video project with others? This chapter shows you how to export your finished video.

Scuba Diving

Click on image to see video

disc

UNDERSTANDING PREMIERE OUTPUT

You can output your video projects into a variety of formats. The output method you choose determines what options are available. This section gives you an overview of the numerous ways you can output your video creation.

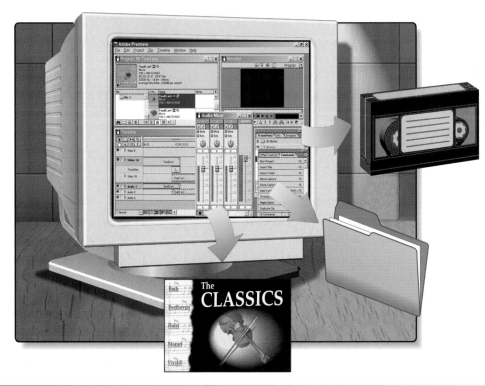

Project Settings

When you selected your project's settings at the beginning of your video's production, you determined characteristics such as frame size and compression. Premiere applies these same settings during output unless you specify otherwise. To learn more about the different project settings available, see Chapter 2.

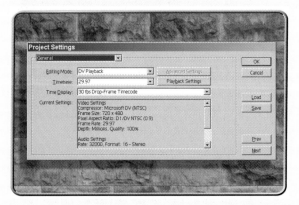

Output Options

You can choose to output your project from either the Timeline or from a clip. When outputting from the Timeline window, you can export either the entire project or a portion of the work area. When outputting from a clip, you can export the entire clip or just the portion between the in and out points. For more information on in and out points, see Chapter 7.

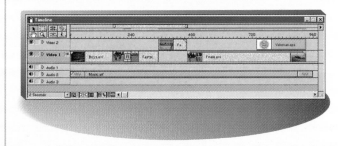

Output to Videotape

You can use the Print to Video or the Export to Tape commands to output to videotape. The method you choose depends on your hardware configuration. You can record directly onto a tape recorder device, such as a DV camcorder or a DV deck. Premiere lets you use device control or operate the recording device manually.

Output for the Web

You can export your video to the Web with a little help from three plug-in programs that come with Premiere 6: Media Cleaner EZ, RealMedia Export, and Windows Media. Each plug-in follows a different procedure, so be sure to check each plug-in's documentation to learn about the available features.

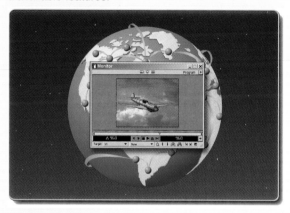

Output to Other File Formats

You can output your project to movie file formats, such as QuickTime or Windows AVI, or to formats used by other programs, such as Adobe After Effects. You can even output a single frame in your video to an image file.

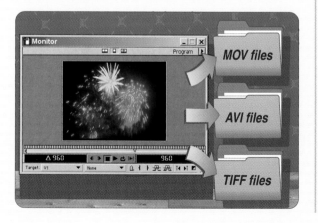

Output to a CD-ROM

When outputting to CD-ROM, you must consider the type of CD-ROM drive the intended audience is using, compatibility issues, file size, and playback. For older CD-ROM drives, set the exported file to play at a lower frame rate.

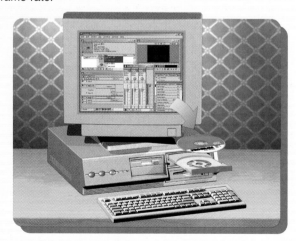

EXPORT TO A MOVIE FILE

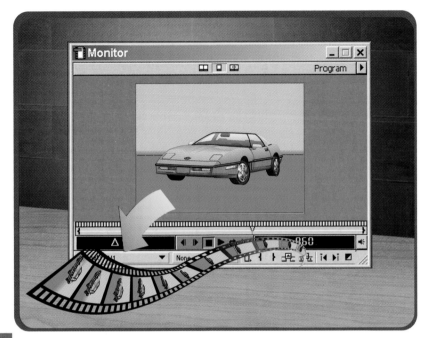

You can export your video, or a part of your video, to a movie file format that a movie player program can display. For example, you may export your project as a QuickTime movie or a Windows AVI movie.

EXPORT TO A MOVIE FILE

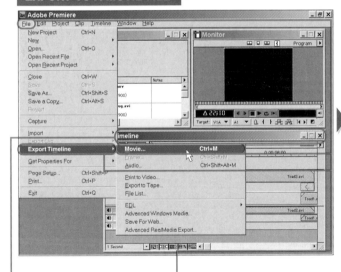

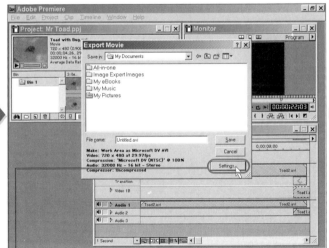

1 Select the Timeline or Monitor window.

■ To export a portion of your video, set the work area over the range in the Timeline window.

Note: See Chapter 6 to learn more about using the Timeline window.

2 Click **File**.

3 Click **Export Timeline**.

4 Click **Movie**.

■ The Export Movie dialog box opens.

5 Click **Settings**.

■ The Export Movie Settings dialog box opens.

Note: See Chapter 2 to learn more about project settings.

Can I export a clip instead of my edited video?

Yes. Open the clip from the Project window and set the in and out points, if needed. Then follow the steps shown below to export the clip as a movie file. To learn more about working with the Clip window, see Chapter 5.

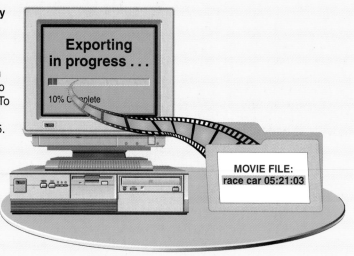

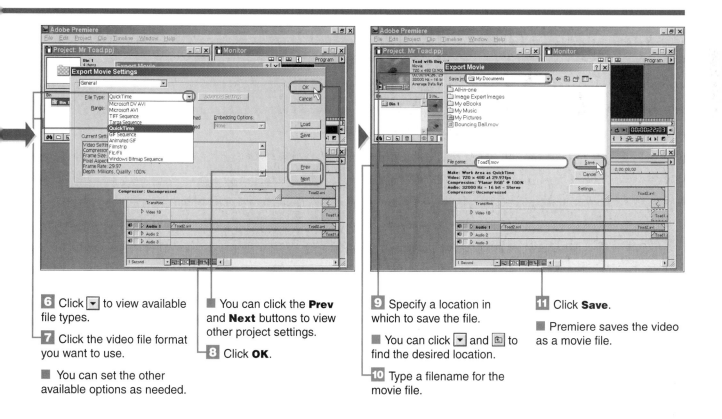

6 Click ▼ to view available file types.

7 Click the video file format you want to use.

■ You can set the other available options as needed.

■ You can click the **Prev** and **Next** buttons to view other project settings.

8 Click **OK**.

9 Specify a location in which to save the file.

■ You can click ▼ and 🖼 to find the desired location.

10 Type a filename for the movie file.

11 Click **Save**.

■ Premiere saves the video as a movie file.

EXPORT A SINGLE FRAME

You can export a single frame or still image from your video project as an image file type that another program can display. For example, you may want to export a frame from your video for use as a GIF graphic on a Web page or to e-mail to a friend.

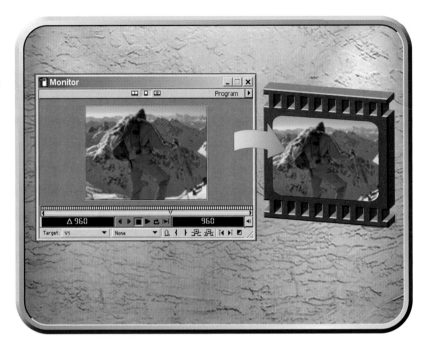

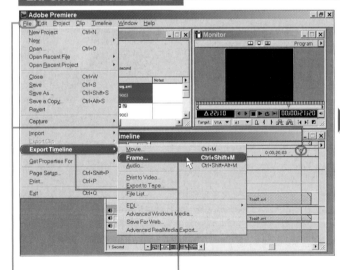

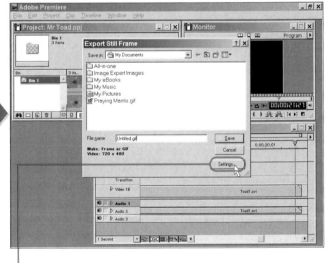

1 Cue the Timeline's edit line to the frame you want to export.

Note: See Chapter 6 to learn more about working with the Timeline.

2 Click **File**.

3 Click **Export Timeline**.

4 Click **Frame**.

■ The Export Still Frame dialog box opens.

5 Click **Settings**.

■ The Export Still Frame Settings dialog box opens.

288

How do I set a frame size for the exported image file?

In the Export Still Frame Settings dialog box, click **Next** or **Prev** to move back and forth between the General, Video Settings, Keyframe and Rendering Options, and Special Processing panels. The Video Settings panel has options for setting frame size. To learn more about project settings, see Chapter 3.

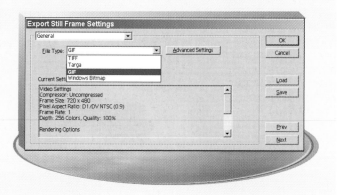

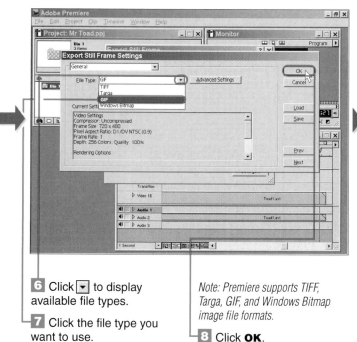

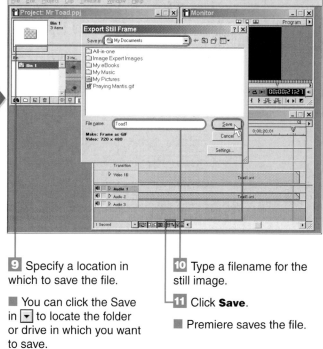

6 Click ▼ to display available file types.

7 Click the file type you want to use.

Note: Premiere supports TIFF, Targa, GIF, and Windows Bitmap image file formats.

8 Click **OK**.

9 Specify a location in which to save the file.

■ You can click the Save in ▼ to locate the folder or drive in which you want to save.

10 Type a filename for the still image.

11 Click **Save**.

■ Premiere saves the file.

EXPORT TO VIDEOTAPE

You can export your video project to a videocassette if your computer system allows you to output video signals and you have a video tape recorder connected to your computer. The simplest method is to use device control in Premiere to record directly onto a DV device using the Export to Tape command.

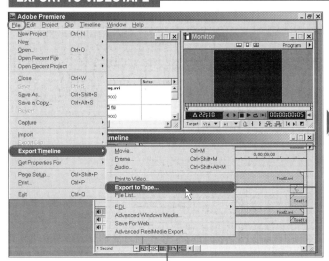

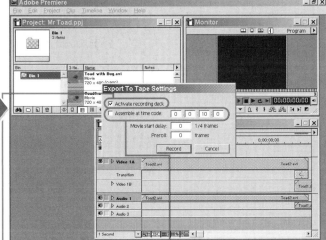

1 Connect the DV device you want to record to, making sure that the device is powered on with a tape inserted.

Note: Most tape recorder devices use a black, coded cassette tape that has a black video signal and timecode.

2 Click **File**.

3 Click **Export Timeline**.

4 Click **Export to Tape**.

■ The Export to Tape Settings dialog box opens.

Note: The options in the dialog box may vary based on the hardware you are using.

5 Click **Activate recording deck** (□ changes to ☑).

■ The record mode for the DV deck or camera is activated.

■ Click here if you want to enter a timecode number to start the recording and type the number.

What does the Print to Video command do?

Use the Print to Video command when you want to operate the recording device manually. Make sure the tape you are recording to is cued and ready to go, then click **File**, **Export Timeline**, and then **Print to Video**. The Print to Video dialog box appears, and you can specify color bar or playback options. When you are ready to record, click **OK** and start the recording device.

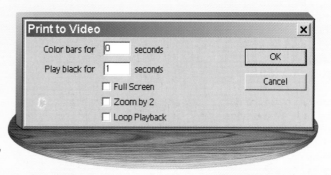

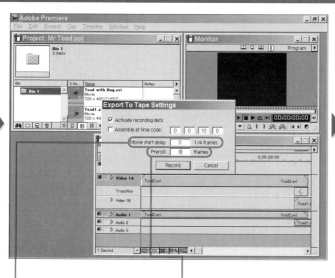

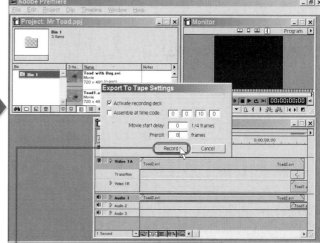

■ Use this option to delay the playback a specified number of quarter-frames.

■ Use this option to specify a number of frames to rewind from the start time to get the tape up to speed.

6 Click **Record**.

■ Playback begins.

■ If you are controlling the recorder device manually, push the Record button on the device.

Note: To stop recording, push the Stop button on the recorder device.

EXPORT FOR THE WEB WITH CLEANER EZ

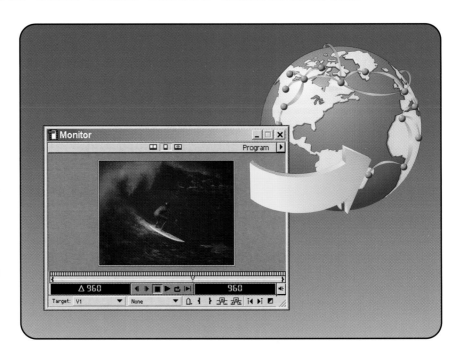

You can output your video for the Web or to an intranet by saving your project as a streaming video file using one of three plug-in programs that come with Premiere. Streaming video is one of the most popular video formats on the Web because it lets users watch the video as it downloads rather than wait for the entire file to download.

EXPORT FOR THE WEB WITH CLEANER EZ

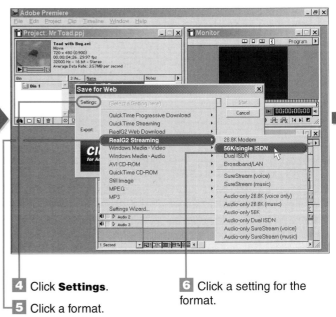

1 Click **File**.

2 Click **Export Timeline**.

3 Click **Save for Web**.

■ The Cleaner EZ plug-in dialog box opens.

Note: Cleaner EZ must be installed for this feature to be available.

4 Click **Settings**.

5 Click a format.

6 Click a setting for the format.

How do I know which plug-in to use?

All three plug-ins will optimize your video for the Web. Use the RealNetworks plug-in to create RealVideo formats. Use the Advanced Windows Media plug-in to output in WMV format for Windows Media Player version 7 and higher. The Cleaner EZ plug-in can create QuickTime or Windows streaming media.

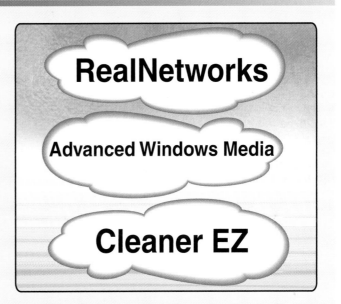

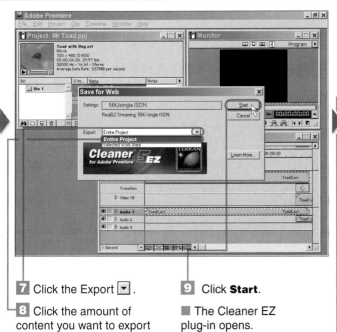

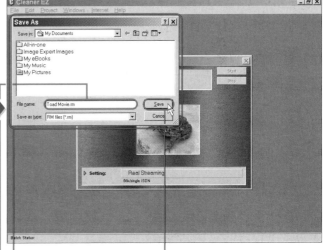

7 Click the Export ▾ .

8 Click the amount of content you want to export

9 Click **Start**.

■ The Cleaner EZ plug-in opens.

■ Based on the chosen format, Cleaner EZ prompts you to either save the file or enter a server name to which it should export.

10 Type the necessary information for server or filename.

11 Click **Save**.

Note: Consult the plug-in documentation to find help with using the plug-in.

■ Cleaner EZ saves the video in the specified format.

INDEX

INDEX

INDEX

Read Less – Learn More™

Visual

Simplified®

Simply the Easiest Way to Learn

For visual learners who are brand-new to a topic and want to be shown, not told, how to solve a problem in a friendly, approachable way.

All *Simplified*® books feature friendly Disk characters who demonstrate and explain the purpose of each task.

Title	ISBN	Price
America Online® Simplified®, 2nd Ed.	0-7645-3433-5	$27.99
Computers Simplified®, 5th Ed.	0-7645-3524-2	$27.99
Creating Web Pages with HTML Simplified®, 2nd Ed.	0-7645-6067-0	$27.99
Excel 97 Simplified®	0-7645-6022-0	$27.99
FrontPage® 2000 Simplified®	0-7645-3450-5	$27.99
Internet and World Wide Web Simplified®, 3rd Ed.	0-7645-3409-2	$27.99
Microsoft® Access 2000 Simplified®	0-7645-6058-1	$27.99
Microsoft® Excel 2000 Simplified®	0-7645-6053-0	$27.99
Microsoft® Office 2000 Simplified®	0-7645-6052-2	$29.99
Microsoft® Word 2000 Simplified®	0-7645-6054-9	$27.99
More Windows® 95 Simplified®	1-56884-689-4	$27.99
More Windows® 98 Simplified®	0-7645-6037-9	$27.99
Office 97 Simplified®	0-7645-6009-3	$29.99
PC Upgrade and Repair Simplified®, 2nd Ed.	0-7645-3560-9	$27.99
Windows® 95 Simplified®	1-56884-662-2	$27.99
Windows® 98 Simplified®	0-7645-6030-1	$27.99
Windows® 2000 Professional Simplified®	0-7645-3422-X	$27.99
Windows® Me Millennium Edition Simplified®	0-7645-3494-7	$27.99
Word 97 Simplified®	0-7645-6011-5	$27.99

Over 10 million *Visual* books in print!